The

GARDENER'S COTTAGE

IN RIVERSIDE, ILLINOIS

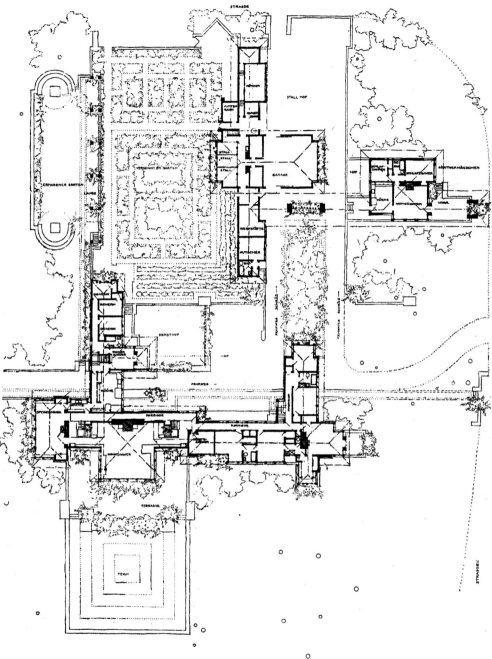

AVERY COONLEY HOUSE, RIVERSIDE, ILL., 1908: GROUND PLAN.

The Gardener's Cottage (upper right) completed the design of the entire Coonley estate, a National Historic Landmark in the Riverside Historic District. From the Wasmuth Portfolio, a German-language edition.

The
GARDENER'S COTTAGE

IN RIVERSIDE, ILLINOIS

LIVING IN A "SMALL MASTERPIECE" by FRANK LLOYD WRIGHT,
JENS JENSEN, and FREDERICK LAW OLMSTED

Cathy Jean Maloney

CENTER BOOKS ON CHICAGO AND ENVIRONS
GEORGE F. THOMPSON, SERIES FOUNDER AND DIRECTOR

THE CENTER FOR AMERICAN PLACES
AT COLUMBIA COLLEGE CHICAGO

For Mike and Thomas

CONTENTS

Acknowledgments IX

The Gardener's Cottage 3

In Their Nature: The Coonleys Discover Riverside 9

Riverside, Illinois, a National Historic District

Frederick Law Olmsted, Landscape Architect

A Meeting of the Minds: Prairie Schools in Riverside 21

Conservation and Chicago's Prairie Schools

The Gardener and His Wife 29

Leaving the Riverside Villa 35

After Archie Gill, Gardener

Be It Ever So Humble 41

Frank Lloyd Wright's Small Homes and Cottages

A Landscape Legacy 67

Jens Jensen, Landscape Architect

Living in the Gardener's Cottage 85

Notes 101

About the Author 107

ACKNOWLEDGMENTS

MY FAMILY WOULD NOT have the pleasure of living in the Gardener's Cottage had it not been for the stewardship of preservation-minded individuals over the past century. Prior owners of the Gardener's Cottage in historic Riverside, Illinois, have lovingly maintained the structure and enhanced the surrounding grounds and landscape. Avery and Queene Ferry Coonley are to be remembered for their willingness to extend beauty into the design of a working family's home. Subsequent owners, including Peter E. Kroehler, the Arthur Benwitz family, Mr. and Mrs. Paul Holt, Susan Shipper-Smith, Dr. Theodore Smith and Dorothy Schroeder, and Mary Ann and John Crayton, each contributed to the present-day charm of the cottage.

I am forever thankful to the many librarians and archivists who helped me navigate the dusty tomes during my historical research. My sincere thanks go to the staff at the University of Michigan's Bentley Library, Frank Lloyd Wright Research Center in Oak Park, Illinois, Getty Research Institute in Los Angeles, Frank Lloyd Wright Foundation at Taliesen West in Scottsdale, Arizona, Riverside Historical Society, Riverside Public Library, and Sterling Morton Library at the Morton Arboretum in Lisle, Illinois.

Mrs. Virginia Henry was especially helpful in sharing her memories and photos of the Gardener's Cottage in the early days. The late Jerry Kumery was most gracious in lending his expertise and artistry to photograph the cottage's garden, birds, and wildlife. My colleagues at the Morton Arboretum were extremely helpful in providing historical and horticultural advice. Scott Mehaffey, formerly the arboretum's landscape architect, was particularly supportive. The team at the Center for American Places at Columbia College Chicago was invaluable in helping me bring this story to light. My family, as always, deserves my thanks and love for such support and inspiration.

—C. J. M.
The Gardener's Cottage
Riverside, Illinois
Autumnal Equinox 2009

The
GARDENER'S COTTAGE

IN RIVERSIDE, ILLINOIS

THE GARDENER'S COTTAGE

WE'D KNOWN ABOUT the so-called Gardener's Cottage for years, but the newly listed real estate ad hooked us:

> For Sale: The Gardener's Cottage: A small masterpiece presented by three great American titans: Frederick Law Olmsted, Frank Lloyd Wright, and Jens Jensen.

We were familiar with Olmsted, having lived in Riverside for more than eighteen years. On one of many house-hunting missions, my husband, Mike, and I stumbled upon this historic village, an 1869 planned community designed by the "Father of American Landscape Architecture," Frederick Law Olmsted, and his professional partner, architect Calvert Vaux, that is listed on the United States Register of Historic Places. Then newlyweds renting a charming coach house in Chicago's North Side, we felt the lure of home ownership. Driving south down Harlem Avenue, noting strip mall after strip mall, we both felt discouraged and certain that nothing good would come of this expedition.

We were so wrong. As soon as we turned into Riverside, we knew we were home. Even today, the timeless beauty of Olmsted and Vaux's creation continues to amaze and delight. Its pioneering design, borrowed from and embracing nature, has survived decades of "progress" and change. Surrounded by shopping malls, a huge quarry, and busy highways, bracketed and bisected by railroads, beneath major flight patterns, Riverside nonetheless offers an oasis of otherworldly serenity. Encircled by the Des Plaines River and buffered by forest preserves, the charm of

Riverside's winding streets and planned green space offers a refuge from hurly-burly Chicago, a scant ten miles away.

Many have been captivated by Olmsted and Vaux's vision. Mike and I are still considered newcomers in this historic village, where families count back three and four generations. As Riverside's magic worked on us, our gardening hobbies developed into avocations. Mike became our household expert on vegetable growing, while I focused on ornamentals and design. I started researching and writing about garden history in regional and national publications and worked with some of Chicago's leading horticultural organizations.

We soon discovered Jens Jensen (1860–1951), the "Dean of American Landscape Architecture," according to *The New York Times* at the time of his death. With eyes better trained to recognize good landscape design, we now appreciated Jensen's work in the Chicago Parks and in Wisconsin's Door County, one of our favorite haunts. Jensen's naturalistic designs and use of native plants reminded me of childhood walks in Cook County Forest Preserves and of adventures with my sister and brothers in the nearby prairie and woods. Mike and I learned of Chicago's Prairie Club, an early conservation group of which Jensen was a founder, and ultimately we became members and directors of the club's various boards. To celebrate the club's heritage, I wrote a pictorial history, *The Prairie Club of Chicago*. We later bought a little cabin in the club's historic dune front camp in Michigan. From Jensen neophytes we became proper prairie proponents.

Then there was Frank Lloyd Wright (1867–1959). This world-famous architect is a household name in Chicago and much of the world. At this point, however, we were not Wrightophiles. I loved Victorian eclectic architecture and English cottages. Mike did enjoy Wrightian style—he secretly longed for simple lines and sparse furnishings amidst my penchant for burled wood and carved fretwork. Having lived for a while with his aunt and uncle in their lovely Bruce Goff home, Mike appreciated a modern style. We liked Wright homes but weren't sure they were right for us.

Yet, how could we resist looking at the Gardener's Cottage? What was the result when "three great American titans" collided? And what of the poor gardener, for heaven's sake, for whom the home was named? Originally, this was his humble home, part of an estate designed circa 1907 for Wright's clients, Avery and Queene Ferry Coonley. Mr. Coonley, a charter member of many early conservationist

The view across the treetops of Riverside to downtown Chicago captures the dense greenery envisioned by Frederick Law Olmsted. Photo by the author, 2008.

Today, the Des Plaines River is a short walk from the Gardener's Cottage and, as in Olmsted and Vaux's General Plan of 1869, continues to enhance the community with its natural beauty. Photo by the author, 2009.

groups, and Mrs. Coonley, daughter of renowned seedsman Dexter M. Ferry, surely had opinions about flowers. Wright was not shy about his views of organic architecture, nor was Jensen a wallflower when it came to landscape design. How did the beleaguered gardener go about his duties with these strong-willed artists underfoot?

We called our realtor, who was properly dumbfounded. After all, we had just moved into another house in Riverside less than a year before. This would be our fourth house in Riverside, after an English cottage, a Georgian, and a "French Eclectic." Never ones to let moss grow under our feet, our family moved rather than remodeled but always within Riverside. After all of these moves, the realization hit that, as long as a house had character, the *views* from the home were much more important than the building itself. There are so many beautiful vistas in Riverside, couldn't we find a view that was characteristically Riversidian, with green space and maybe, just possibly, a slice of river or forest preserve? Otherwise, I thought, our house might as well be located in any other of Chicago's hundreds of suburbs.

Mike says he knew the house was for us the minute he stepped in the door. I wasn't so sure. I confess I felt a bit like Bilbo Baggins upon first entering the Gardener's Cottage—it was, as our realtor spoke in realtor-speak, "cozy." I guess we were ready for cozy: through summers at our Prairie Club cabin we'd discovered that our family of three managed quite well in modest quarters. Whether a call for simplicity or, maybe, the house actually called to us, we were prepared to pare down. The deal was sealed for me when I first saw the historical garden drawings and plant lists left by the sellers. A framed planting plan, signed by Jens Jensen and dated 1913, showed his vision for the estate's grounds, and our home-to-be was clearly labeled the Gardener's Cottage. The sellers were dedicated gardeners who had transformed the grounds with native plantings. And the views! From every window I saw classic views of Riverside: greenery, curving roads, and a sparkle of river. This was a cottage truly meant for gardeners.

We sold almost all of our furniture. The antiques we had collected over the years simply didn't fit, stylistically or physically. Friends and family, used to our constant moves, scratched their heads. The editing of possessions was hard, until we realized we had boxes and boxes labeled "Memories," of which we had no memory. Time for a fresh start! We moved in early spring, and the adventure began.

We soon discovered that the cottage had its own ethos that quietly beckoned. Its simplicity of form and materials worked into our own lifestyle. Its small footprint made a big impression on our hearts. Questions formed: Why did the affluent Coonleys, who could have chosen any site in the Chicago area, settle here? Why did they build such a nice abode, the Gardener's Cottage, for hired help? How did the beauty of the site, carved from nature some three decades earlier by Olmsted and Vaux, inspire Wright and Jensen? Who was the gardener, and how might he have enjoyed this home? How did the gardens around the cottage and the larger estate affect those within?

My search began with the people and extended to the plants. Welcome to the Gardener's Cottage and its gardens.

IN THEIR NATURE
THE COONLEYS DISCOVER RIVERSIDE

SEVERAL OLD CHESTNUTS chronicle how the many colorful characters converged in creating the Coonley estate. Frank Lloyd Wright's autobiography offers the oft-quoted "countenance of character" inherent in his work that allegedly propelled the Coonleys to his office. Kindred spirits, the Coonleys' eclectic intellectual pursuits were succinctly captured in Avery Coonley's fabled rejection of vegetarianism as one "ism" too many after being Christian Scientists, Wright homeowners, women's suffragettes, and progressive educators.[1] These shopworn tales are pale impressions of the very rich personalities involved in creating this National Historic Landmark home. Avery and Queene Coonley, both of prominent and wealthy families, chose Riverside for their unorthodox home, and through their diverse interests in the arts, education, and environmental fields they brought a pageant of interesting people and ideas to the little railroad village. They lived here only about ten years, but their legacy has lasted for decades.

Queene Ferry Coonley (1874–1958) was the youngest of four children born to Dexter Mason Ferry and Addie Miller. Gardening was an integral part of Queene's life from birth. The Detroit-based family business, Ferry Seed Company, grew from an early partnership her father formed in 1856 to one of the largest seedhouses in the world.

Queene inherited both a sense of innovation and good business from her father as well as an appreciation for the outdoors. "Ladies should cultivate flowers as an invigorating and inspiring out-door occupation. Many are pining and dying from monotony and depression, who might bury their cares by planting a few seeds . . . ," wrote D. M. Ferry in his *1876 Seed Annual*, when Queene was three years old.[2] Queene Ferry enjoyed travel, art, and the luxuries of her position, but when faced with adversity, such as the early death of her husband and financial concerns during the Depression, she rose to the occasion. "[My hands] were made for good hard work, Father used to tell me," she wrote to brother Dexter in the 1930s, "and are somewhat in the pattern of Father's."[3]

Queene graduated from Vassar College in 1896 with an intended career of teaching elementary school. Her love of Vassar and education were lifelong passions. With her sister, Blanche, Queene endowed Vassar's Alumni House and served on its Board of Trustees. She supported many philanthropic causes, including women's rights and settlement houses, but progressive education was a particular interest. She founded two *avant garde* schools in the Chicago area, beginning with the "cottage school" on her own Riverside grounds.[4] Her education philosophy, which she and Avery endorsed for their own daughter, Elizabeth, embraced experiential learning, including immersion in the outdoors, practical arts, readings and dramatic interpretations of classic literature, and other ideals associated with the Progressive Era. The linkage with nature was so successful at the Cottage School that it was cited for excellence by John Dewey, then America's foremost progressive educator: "The Cottage School at Riverside, Ill . . . put a great deal of stress on their nature study work . . . the children have a garden where they plant early and late vegetables, so that they can use them for their cooking class in the spring and fall; the pupils do all the work here, plant, weed and gather the things."[5]

Writing in *Progressive Education* in 1927, Mrs. Coonley described an ideal school which, while unidentified, is likely her cottage school in Riverside:

> In so far as possible, we should place schools in open and country settings . . . I once knew such a group who selected a choice area on the edge of a village on a winding river. This river was one of the bi-annual stopping places of the migratory birds. It made for endless lessons in geography, it was associated with the days of the early French explorers and was a section rich in stories of thrilling adventure of Indian days. It skirted woods rich in wild flowers and native blossoming trees; the spot selected for the school buildings was where the wild crab-apple trees made such an ecstasy of beauty when in blossom, that had it been in Japan, pilgrimages would have been made across the entire country to contemplate such beauty.[6]

SCENE ON D. M. FERRY & CO'S SEED FARM.   Weeding Cabbage.

Women's work ca. 1881 on Queene Ferry's father's farm. The American Rural Home, *March 10, 1881, from the author's collection.*

A dinner break in the fields at Ferry Farm. The American Rural Home, *March 17, 1881, from the author's collection.*

Photograph of the Des Plaines River, ca. 1910, a haven for wildlife. Photographer unknown. From the author's collection.

Riverside residents enjoyed the recreational and educational aspects of the river (ca. 1910). Photographer unknown. From the author's collecton.

Avery Coonley (1870–1920) was the second oldest of six children born to John Clark Coonley and Lydia Arms Avery Coonley, of Chicago. The Coonley home was in a well-to-do neighborhood on the near North Side. Although they were raised in a city environment, the young Coonley family reveled in the outdoors at their ancestral summer home, Hillside, in Wyoming, New York. There, the children frolicked in the fields, gathered fruits and flowers, and became expert equestrians. The eldest son, Avery, and his younger brothers, Howard, Prentiss, and John, were active in their father's multi-faceted manufacturing businesses. Educated at Harvard, Avery's career choices and artistic sensibilities were strongly influenced by the home-based teaching from his mother, Lydia Avery Coonley, herself a suffragette and author. To promote literary appreciation among her children, Lydia Coonley offered five cents per stanza for any original verse. The young Avery took up the challenge and produced such tongue-in-cheek lyrics as follows, along with his invoice payable to the "Avery Coonley Poetry Company:"

An Inspiration
I've got to have just five cents more;
A rhyme! My sakes, a rhyme!
I can't make squirrel rhyme with whirl,
But wait, just give me time.

There's biscuit, but what rhymes with it?
Alas, for my poor purse!
I know—I'm on to Shakespeare's trick!
I'll write it in blank verse.[7]

Lydia Coonley was also a devotee of nature and often wrote of its charms in various literary magazines and books. As reported in *Chronicles of an American Home*, Avery produced a "sly burlesque on his mother's habit of personifying the lesser works of Nature" in another poem entitled, "A Garden-Truck Revery."[8] He later turned his writing talents to publish the *Little Chronicle*, a weekly news magazine for schoolchildren and, still later, to manage communications for the Christian Science church.

On June 8, 1901, Queene Ferry and Avery Coonley, aged twenty-seven and thirty respectively, were married in Unadilla, New York, a pleasant town in the foothills of the Catskill Mountains, where the Ferry family maintained a summer home and farm, Milfer. These two American families had many common interests and backgrounds, including Ivy League educations, philanthropic causes, art appreciation, and, most important for the Riverside estate, an abiding love of nature. The families supported each other in many ways: sharing their summer homes, vacation trips, and, occasionally, investment opportunities. Fellow nature lovers and suffragettes, Queene Ferry and Lydia Avery Coonley Ward shared many interests. Throughout the decades, Queene's correspondence speaks highly of "Mother Coonley," whose friends included Susan B. Anthony and social settlement Hull House founder, Jane Addams.

Although family members got along well together, they did not see eye to eye on everything. Avery and Queene were freethinkers, even among families of independent minds. In politics, for example, the Avery Coonleys vigorously supported Teddy Roosevelt in 1912, even while brother Dexter Ferry, who, like his father, was involved in politics, worked for Howard Taft.[9] Unafraid of taking unpopular stances in the interest of their beliefs, the young Coonley couple's conversion to the Christian Scientist religion particularly caused discord within the normally tight-knit family. Changing religions required that Queene Ferry's name be dropped from the rolls of the family's Congregational church in Detroit. In 1905, Queene asked her brother, Dexter—then serving in the Michigan House of Representatives—to intercede on her behalf. Brother Ferry referred to general anti-Christian Science feelings in Detroit and opined that her religious conversion would seriously sadden their parents' declining years. He closed his letter with the note, "Consider this carefully and if your mind and body both actually need another faith and religion try to confine the disturbance to Chicago where it apparently hurts less and thereby allow us here in Detroit live in peace."[10] Clearly, Avery and Queene, once committed to a cause, would follow their hearts and minds despite family or social pressures. This independent spirit helps to explain their selection of iconoclastic designers such as Frank Lloyd Wright and Jens Jensen.

The newlywed Coonleys had moved to Chicago, where they joined brother John Coonley in the Hyde Park neighborhood.[11] Queene recalled: "The settling of your first home after you are married is a unique experience. To my last day I shall remember Avery's and my fun settling our little Woodlawn Avenue house."[12] These housekeeping details would keep Queene Ferry busy while Avery worked long hours at business. Certainly in Hyde Park, Queene would also have had contact with the University of Chicago's scholar John Dewey, whose progressive "lab school" paved the way nationwide for new approaches in holistic education. The fledgling university, incorporated in 1890, was also then home to John Merle Coulter and Henry C. Cowles, whose pioneering work in botany and ecology was making headlines. These leaders in education and conservation perhaps further influenced the Coonleys' commitment to education and, later, to the naturalistic landscapes espoused by Jensen.

On December 3, 1902, the Coonleys welcomed their daughter, Elizabeth Ferry Coonley, into the world. Shortly thereafter in 1904, perhaps reflecting the need for more spacious quarters in the countryside or perhaps to join brother Howard Coonley and his family, the Coonleys moved to Riverside.[13] They lived for a while on Herrick Road before buying land on Bloomingbank Road. Although their Bloomingbank homesite was undeveloped, the Coonleys clearly saw the potential in its beautiful vistas and proximity to the woods and Des Plaines River. Like many others before and after them, the Coonleys savored the privilege of living in Frederick Law Olmsted's nature-inspired community. The marriage of the Coonley and Ferry families brought together two nature lovers, now irrepressibly drawn to the beauty of the outdoors in Riverside.

*Then, as now, the Des Plaines River offers fishing and hikes along woodland trails.
Photos by the author, 2004.*

Deer in the forest in historic Riverside. Photo by Tom Maloney, 2004.

Riverside, Illinois, a National Historic District

LIKE MANY INVESTMENT groups in the late 1860s, the Riverside Improvement Company comprised a group of East Coast businessmen who hoped to capitalize on Chicago's hot real estate market and burgeoning commuter railroad system. The Riverside investors hired nationally renowned landscape architect, Frederick Law Olmsted, and his architect partner, Calvert Vaux. Their forward-thinking plan for the village emphasized copious green space, graciously curved walkways and streets, and harmony with existing natural features. Olmsted hoped to improve social conditions and engender civility by creating such communities that celebrated nature.

Olmsted's firm had been commissioned at about the same time to develop a plan for Chicago's south park system. As in many major cities, Chicagoans were awakening to the healthful benefits of green space as an antidote to the crushing conditions of industrialization. Olmsted, having worked throughout the United States, was underwhelmed by Chicago's natural prairie scenery. His 1868 preliminary report to the Riverside investors characterized Chicago's environs as generally uninteresting and "positively dreary." Olmsted declared the potential Riverside site, once farmland, as one with "natural advantages" much beyond any other. Thanks to the Des Plaines River, which surrounds Riverside on two sides, and existing groves of native trees, Olmsted approved the potential of the site.

The Olmsted and Vaux General Plan of 1869 emphasized green space—with more than half of the village's original 1,600 acres devoted to public parks or islands of green at the curved intersections of winding streets. Still, in his preliminary report, Olmsted cautioned investors that it could not be a "Village in a Park," as their marketing slogans promised, piggybacking on the bankable effects of parkland on real estate. Naturalistic parks, in Olmsted's view, should completely subordinate buildings and the "hand of man," whereas Riverside must accommodate dwellings and other signs of domesticity. The Olmsted and Vaux design proposed thirty-foot setbacks from the street to obscure "ugly and inappropriate houses," and it included a requirement for homeowners to plant two or three trees between their house and the road.

Many of Riverside's curvilinear streets were named by Olmsted and reflect his interest and homage to nature and literature. Thus, Michaux Road intersects with Bartram Road, which later joins Nuttall Road, commemorating the famous early naturalists André Michaux, John and William Bartram, and Thomas Nuttall. Downing and

Audubon roads converge on the Long common and honor American horticulturist Andrew Jackson Downing and naturalist John James Audubon. Shenstone and Addison roads note Olmsted's respect for English literary artists William Shenstone and Joseph Addison. Olmsted designed these winding roads to emulate the naturally sinuous path of the Des Plaines River—and also to discourage fast-paced commercial traffic.

Despite Olmsted's distaste of architectural infringements on nature, many noted architects created homes in Riverside. Louis Sullivan, Frank Lloyd Wright, and William Le Baron Jenney were among the architects represented. But it was Olmsted's pioneering design, interweaving green space throughout the community, which made the village unique. In 1970, the entire Village of Riverside was designated a National Historic District: as the National Historic District application notes, "Riverside is the nation's first development arranged so that open spaces and parkland are integral parts of the daily urban environment."

Today, as in the past, residents savor the proximity of nature in their daily lives. It is common, on a crisp autumn day or a sparkling spring morning, for neighbors to meet neighbors, who often exclaim, "Aren't we lucky to live here!" One year our family kept a nature journal and recorded sightings of beavers, blue heron, coyote, kingfishers, migratory songbirds, osprey, owls, red fox, river otters, and the ever-present deer. Mike, our son, Tom, and I will never forget surprising a ten-point buck paused while crossing a rocky part of the river. It was like a picture postcard from northern Wisconsin, but it was here in Riverside, a scant ten miles from Chicago's Loop. Thanks to decades of careful stewardship, most of Riverside's green space and natural features have been preserved. Olmsted's classic design continues to delight and inspire generation after generation.

Frederick Law Olmsted, Landscape Architect

FREDERICK LAW OLMSTED (1822–1903) revolutionized American garden design and, through his prodigious high-profile work, is the acknowledged "Father of American Landscape Architecture." Although other individuals pioneered this fledgling discipline (notably, Andrew Jackson Downing, 1815–1852), Olmsted's work received national attention and support through hundreds of his major implemented landscape designs in municipal pleasure grounds, national parks, cemeteries, academic campuses, and private estates. Among his most famous works are New York's Central and Prospect parks; the United States Capitol Grounds; park systems in Boston, Buffalo, and Chicago; Stanford University; Yosemite Valley; and the 1893 World's Fair in Chicago.

Prior to Olmsted's contributions, mid-Victorian American gardens were largely influenced by European trends, faddish new plant novelties, and the advice of the nearest nurseryman. Horticultural journals tended to be plant-focused, with more cultural advice than hints on garden design. If a homeowner had sufficient wealth to warrant an ornamental garden in addition to a kitchen garden, he might hire a gardener who typically hailed from England, Ireland, or Scotland with experience in the design styles and plants of those nations, as opposed to America's regional nuances.

Olmsted emphasized the total landscape composition, not just combinations of plants. With his patchwork formal education, Olmsted's early travels in the New England countryside with his family, and later across America and Europe, informed his design philosophies. His extensive reading of literary classics and of naturalists' writings also influenced his art. Olmsted looked to nature for inspiration in his designs, and he proposed that humanmade elements be subservient to the charms of natural beauty. Rejecting the Victorian carpet bedding craze, which relied upon the latest colorful annual flowers, Olmsted's landscapes were subdued, sublime, and naturalistic.

Olmsted's theories of landscape design were interwoven with his ideals for a more civilized society. He thought that living amidst tastefully landscaped grounds would encourage gentility and reduce the anxiety associated with urban life of the late 1800s. In his preliminary report on Riverside, Olmsted noted, "It is an established conclusion . . . that the mere proximity of dwellings which characterizes all strictly urban neighborhoods, is a prolific source of morbid conditions of the body and mind . . . ." Relief, he decided, could be found in the beauty of nature.

A MEETING OF THE MINDS
PRAIRIE SCHOOLS IN RIVERSIDE

WHEN THE COONLEYS moved to Riverside in the early 1900s, the village had prospered despite occasional ups and downs. The village's initial speculative development had ended in financial woes, complicated by Chicago's Great Fire of 1871. Nonetheless, the small hamlet grew steadily, with a reputation among local artists and nature lovers as an idyllic haven. During the Coonleys' sojourn in Riverside, the population grew steadily from 800 in 1900 to about 4,700 in the mid-1920s. The village was an upscale enclave, but it did not have the social cache of Chicago's North Shore.

Olmsted had designated subdivisions within the village, with the so-called First Division (where the Coonley house was built) located in the southwest peninsula formed by the bend of the Des Plaines River. Residential lots were first sold in this prime area as well as along the broad Longcommon Road, which runs diagonally through the village. Commercial space was planned near the railroad line. During the Coonley era, the village business district sported a hardware store, shoe store, the Riverside Salted Almond Company, a "modern, sanitary" barber shop, bank, and various professional offices. The Riverside Livery offered carriages for weddings, parties, or funerals as well as boarding stables for horses. G. A. Switzer's Pharmacy ran ads in the local paper inviting customers to "Drink and Fear Not: Our Syrups and Fruit Juices are Pure and Wholesome . . . ."[1] A. R. Owen General Store sold Dutchess apples, fresh-roasted peanuts, homegrown cucumbers, homemade sausage ("made only from fresh pork and spices in our own kitchen"), Illinois Elberta peaches, Kalamazoo celery, melons, Mountain Bartlett pears, pie plant, spring ducks from the country, and stewing chickens. In season, strawberries were ten cents a quart, apples seventy-five cents a peck, asparagus fifteen cents a bunch, and sweet navel oranges ranged from nineteen to forty-five cents per dozen. While shopping in Riverside supplied basic needs, Mrs. Coonley, like many other society ladies, was a frequent patron of Marshall Fields and other upscale stores in downtown Chicago.

The Coonleys kept a relatively low profile in Riverside, as compared to other wealthy families who were frequently featured in the local society pages. News accounts, if at all, mentioned the Coonleys sharing educational opportunities they had secured for Elizabeth and the other 100 or so students of their Cottage School. Occasional newspaper reports mentioned masques and other dramatic performances at the Coonley estate, which became a de facto cultural venue for the village. In January 1913, the *Riverside News* described a Coonley-sponsored performance by naturalist Charles Kellogg for both public and private schools of Riverside.[2] Again in 1913, the *Riverside News* reported that "the Greek Play and Olympian Games given by the pupils of Miss Ward's school on the grounds of Avery Coonley on Decoration Day were extremely interesting."[3] Another report in 1915 described "a very pleasant musical hour was enjoyed at the Cottage School Building . . . Avery Coonley has placed a very nice grand piano there . . . It is truly ideal that [our] community may have such a place for literary and musical pastime and culture. It should inspire effort and appreciation."[4]

Queene Coonley became engrossed in her efforts to enhance education and in her work as a Christian Science practitioner. She and Elizabeth also traveled extensively, with Avery to accompany them as business allowed. Avery was endorsed by the *Riverside News* for a second term as a Cook County Commissioner on the Progressive ticket, being described as possessing an "able mind of sound judgment and considerable experience in many directions . . . unimpeachable integrity; should be re-elected."[5]

Avery was particularly involved in early conservation efforts. He worked on the Des Plaines River Committee, an early environmental group, and he was a charter member of Riverside's local Wildflower Preservation Society.[6] He found a unique way to combine his social settlement work and environmentalism in 1914. "Make War on Dandelions," blared the headline in the *Riverside News*, with the subhead, "Avery Coonley Puts Large Number of Men at Work and Others Help the Movement."[7] The report continued:

An interesting plan to subdue the dandelion and at the same time relieve the labor situation is being given its first trial in Riverside . . . . The fact that there are hundreds of good, hard-working men now out of employment suggested to the management of Gads Hill Center [a settlement house] that they might be used for an overwhelming campaign against the dandelion. A start was made in the west end of the First Division, on the Coonley's lawn with five men on Tuesday, and on Wednesday other residents had become interested and thirteen men were at work. More can be put on later as needed. They use double-pointed asparagus knives with which they cut off the root—below the surface, with the least possible disturbance to the ground.

Love of nature was a consistent theme throughout the Coonleys' life. They embraced nature, as had Olmsted before them, as a source of inspiration, comfort, and learning. Their correspondence often mentions the pastoral beauty not only of Riverside, but of their family homes at Milfer and Hillside and the lessons gleaned from nature there.[8] Elizabeth was tutored in nature in her backyard and in her travels. Reflecting on Elizabeth's education, Queene Ferry wrote, "Avery and I have accented the quiet summers on farms or in the country, with first hand knowledge of nature and home activities, and first hand thinking."[9] This love of nature surely factored into their decision to hire Frank Lloyd Wright and, later, Jens Jensen, to design their home and grounds.

The Coonleys, with their many social contacts, could have chosen any number of architects and landscape architects for their home in Riverside. In 1890, Avery Coonley's mother, Lydia, had commissioned Chicago Arts and Crafts architects Irving and Allen Pond for her house on Division Street and Lake Shore Drive. Avery's brother, Prentiss Coonley, hired Chicago's North Shore favorite, Howard Van Doren Shaw, for a traditionally formal summer home in Lake Forest. In 1907, about the same time Avery and Queene began their association with Frank Lloyd Wright, Lydia Coonley commissioned the Olmsted firm for landscape designs at the family summer home, Hillside. Thus, and not for lack of alternatives, the Riverside Coonleys purposefully chose the ultimate design duo of prairie architecture and landscape architecture, Frank Lloyd Wright and Jens Jensen.

Both Wright and Jensen brought exciting new ideas to their respective fields. They are each credited as pioneers of the so-called "Prairie Schools"—Wright in architecture and Jensen in landscape architecture. Unlike prevailing design styles, the Prairie School celebrated nature, the environment, and regional nuance.

In this ca. 1910 photograph, the Coonley family enjoys their garden, despite Jens Jensen's objections to its architectural design. Courtesy of the Sterling Morton Library at The Morton Arboretum, Lisle, Illinois.

Wright's homes were carefully planned to harmonize organically with the site, and Jensen's landscapes celebrated native plants and naturalistic design.

The Coonleys thought a great deal about the site and nature surrounding their home. In a 1920s retrospective, the *Riverside News* reported:

> They lived here four years studying conditions before they decided to build and make a permanent home. During that time they gathered data on a lot of clever and useful things that could be embodied in a home. This was carefully pasted in a large scrap book.
>
> They selected block two in the First Division, which at that time was a rather unsightly spot. Frank Lloyd Wright, the architect, who had gained an international reputation, was called on to design a place and embody as many of the good things in the scrap book as practical. The best landscape gardner [sic] was employed . . . . No time or money was spared to make this the most beautiful home in Riverside.[10]

While the Coonleys had tremendous input into the shape of their house, the inspired designs from Wright and Jensen have made the home a timeless classic.[11] The Coonleys may have first heard of Frank Lloyd Wright through any number of means. Wright, at the time, was at a particularly tumultuous point in his career. He had already returned from his influential 1905 trip to Japan, but he had not yet embarked on his infamous 1909 trip to Europe with Mamah Cheney, the wife of a client and Wright's future mistress. His work in the Chicago area alone was prodigious. The Tomek house in Riverside, by Wright, was built while the Coonleys lived on Herrick Road. In a 1906 letter to Avery Coonley, Wright referred to this project while he explained his usual rates. His philosophy of creating a holistic design was expressed:

> When we are asked to follow the work into the details of planting, furnishing and decoration (and this I think is the only way the best results are achieved) a fee of 15% on the total cost of these items has been fixed upon . . . I feel that along these lines we are still doing missionary work . . . .[12]

Wright was astute to hold the line on his fees, as the Coonleys were loyal to him throughout the ups and downs of his career. When Wright was in financial straits, the Coonleys were among a handful of supporters who bailed him out. Queene Coonley wrote to her brother, Dexter, in 1911:

> By the way, are you at all interested in Japanese prints? Mr. Wright has, I presume, one of the most interesting collections in the States. He has been collecting for seventeen years. He is selling them now as he says they are too valuable to keep as a personal luxury . . . . Avery and I are spending Friday afternoon in Mr. Wright's studio to have a lesson . . . . If by any chance you are interested in this line, I fancy this is a very unusual opportunity.[13]

Later, in 1935, Mrs. Coonley facilitated an exhibition of Wright's futuristic Broadacre City at the Corcoran Gallery of Art in Washington, D.C. Wright expressed his appreciation with these words in a note to Queene Coonley: "I have never ceased to be grateful and glad that I built the Riverside home of the Coonleys or proud that you thought me worth saving—once upon a time."[14]

On the Coonley project, Jensen was hired after Wright. Like Wright, Jensen was in a particularly busy time of his career, doing private commissions and work for the expanding Chicago park system. The Coonleys had ample opportunities to evaluate Jensen's work. In Riverside, he had landscaped the Henry Babson estate (Louis Sullivan, architect) beginning in 1909. His social circles intersected with those of the Coonleys, his public work in the Chicago parks was well known, and he also landscaped Prentiss Coonley's home in Lake Forest (1910–1911).

Jensen so favorably impressed the Coonleys that they not only hired him for subsequent work (the Downers Grove Kindergarten), but also adopted his causes. Avery Coonley was among nineteen people whom Jensen invited to become charter members of his pioneering conservationist group, Friends of Our Native Landscape. This assembly included such luminaries as poet Harriet Monroe, author Hamlin Garland, ecologist Henry C. Cowles, prairie architect Dwight H. Perkins, and industrialist Stephen Tyng Mather, who became the first director of the National Park Service in 1916.

Jensen and Wright seemed to have a relationship of mutual respect, tinged by a reluctance for two strong egos to share the same space. Letters from Wright to Jensen, from the 1920s through the 1940s, exchange design philosophies that are often at odds with each other. As each headed towards the sunset years of his career, Wright began one letter, "Dear Jens: You dear old Prima Dona [sic]—I don't know whether you exaggerate your own sense of yourself or exaggerate my sense of myself." He goes on to explain his version of the difference between Jensen and himself: "You are a realistic landscapist. I am an abstractionist seeking the pattern behind the realism—the interior structure instead of the comparatively superficial exterior effects you delight in."[15]

Elizabeth Coonley Faulkner remembered a bit of the dynamic between Jensen and Wright as it pertained to the estate's landscape. Recalling that her parents were "very fond of Mr. Jensen," Mrs. Faulkner also remembered where he and Wright may not have seen eye-to-eye on the landscape design. Jensen, for example, objected to the use of non-indigenous evergreens and, in his view, the lack of intimacy in one of the estate's gardens:

> I remember Mr. Jensen chiefly from my mother's affectionate anecdotes about him.… One of them was about the garden in this picture. It had another end corresponding with the end shown, and Mr. Jensen, although I am sure he liked and admired our architect, Frank Lloyd Wright, complained one day of this garden. "It was designed in an architect's office! Look! If I sit at this table, I see the people at the other table and I am afraid that they are having a better time than we are!" He held up his hat to obscure the other table for the rest of the session![16]

Despite this creative tension between Jensen and Wright, the Coonley estate emerged the better for the confluence of these great talents. Building on Olmsted's design for a nature-imbued community, Jensen and Wright developed a perfectly complementary home and landscape.

The Prairie Club hiking in Riverside, 1909. Courtesy of the Westchester Township History Museum, an educational service of Westchester Public Library, Chesterton, Indiana.

Conservation and Chicago's Prairie Schools

CHICAGO'S PRAIRIE SCHOOL of Architecture, featuring Frank Lloyd Wright's organic designs and those of other like-minded architects, is well known. Recently, increased attention has also been paid to Prairie School counterparts in landscape architecture—largely featuring the work of Jens Jensen. Lesser known is the regional conservation movement that both schools inspired.

At the turn of the twentieth century and beyond, Chicago became an unlikely leader in the national battle for environmentalism. Without a recognized treasure, such as Yosemite or Yellowstone, nearby, it may seem curious that Chicagoans were such avid conservationists. But, unlike more mature American urban centers where city limits were already defined, Chicago had a unique opportunity to plan proactively for its burgeoning growth. With the City Beautiful Movement growing out of Chicago's 1893 World's Fair, Chicago's

civic leaders published the Plan of Chicago in 1909, authored by architects D. H. Burnham and Edward H. Bennett. The plan incorporated many ideas from Jensen, Olmsted, and others on the preservation of green spaces in and around Chicago.

In Chicago, at about the time the Coonleys settled in Riverside, environmental groups formed, reflecting a growing national interest in conservation. Local chapters or derivatives of national groups were founded with a distinctly regional focus, such as the Geographic Society of Chicago (1898), the Chicago Ornithological Society (1912), and the Wildflower Preservation Society of Illinois (1913). Jens Jensen was a founding member of two influential groups with a Chicago-based focus: the Friends of Our Native Landscape (1913) and the Prairie Club (1908). The latter hosted weekly hikes around the Chicago countryside to familiarize residents with the wonders of the vanishing wilderness. Friends of Our Native Landscape and the Prairie Club raised awareness for the preservation of a number of state and national parks, and they included members from every walk of life. The groups' achievements include saving the remaining belts of natural areas around Chicago—ultimately resulting in the formation of the Cook County Forest Preserves in 1915.

Scholarly interest in the environment was also headquartered in Chicago while the Coonleys lived in the area. The formal recognition of ecology as a science is often attributed to the pioneering work of John Merle Coulter and Henry C. Cowles of the University of Chicago in the early 1900s. The University's Department of Botany, directed by Coulter and, later, Cowles, highlighted local ecological resources, such as the Indiana Dunes, and argued that their environmental significance ranked among landmark landscapes, such as Yosemite or Yellowstone. The Indiana Dunes became a touchstone around which nascent environmental groups formed.

With support from educated and philanthropic individuals, such as the Coonleys, these organizations thrived and ultimately succeeded in many of their conservation efforts. The harmony-with-nature tenets held by both the architects and landscape architects of the Prairie Schools complemented the goals of the early conservation movements in Chicago, and they were integral to the designs of the Coonley home and grounds.

THE GARDENER AND HIS WIFE

EVEN AS THE COONLEYS and their society friends waged high-profile battles to save the countryside, someone had to weed their backyards. Who was the original gardener of the Gardener's Cottage? Life histories for prominent citizens such as the Coonleys, Wright, and Jensen are fairly easy to find. Much more challenging to discover are biographies of the scores of working men and women who formed the staff of large estates. In an era during which women were rarely mentioned in public records, it's even more unusual to find references to household help.[1]

The 1910 United States Census, the only census covering that snapshot in time when the Coonleys lived in Riverside, sheds some light. In addition to Avery and Queene and their daughter, Elizabeth F., the census lists five servants. There were three unmarried Swedish-born women: thirty-three-year old Carla Albertina, thirty-three-year-old Anna Swanson, who was the cook, and thirty-five-year-old Clara Corkhan, who, in the handwritten parlance of the day, was listed simply as the "Second Girl."[2] These ladies likely lived in the servants' quarters of the main estate. The remaining two servants were Archibald and Susan Gill, an English-born married couple who stayed with the Coonleys through their travels and travails and who seem most likely to be the "Gardener and his Wife." This notion is further supported by later correspondence between Avery Coonley and Wright's apprentice, William Drummond, wherein Coonley and Drummond refer to "Archie's cottage" within the estate. This exchange of letters also mentions the "Stone Cottage" (presumably the Whittlesley cottage), Thornecroft, and Ely's cottage (at 308 Fairbank). By default, Archie's cottage is thus identified as the Gardener's Cottage.[3]

Born in 1877, Archibald Gill was one of six children living with William and Frances Gill of Cornwall, England. The Gills lived in the town of Redruth, known for its mining industries. William Gill and his oldest son, Frederick, were listed as assayers in the 1891 Cornwall census; Archie, then thirteen, was listed as a scholar, as were most young boys still of school age. William Gill died in 1901, when Archie was twenty-four. That same year, according to census notes on immigration, Archibald Gill set sail for the United States, perhaps to support his widowed mother and to seek his own fortune. His future wife, Susan, also emigrated to the U.S. in 1901, although it is unclear if Archie and Susan knew each other in England.[4] They were married in 1905 in Chicago Heights, Illinois. It is also unclear how the Gills were hired by the Coonleys. Susan Gill's obituary notes that Christian Science services were held for her, but whether this religious affiliation was an initial common bond with the Coonleys, or whether Mrs. Gill converted later, is unknown.

Regardless of how the Coonleys came to employ the Gills, we do know that they enjoyed a long relationship, evidencing mutual loyalty and respect. After living in Riverside, the Gills relocated to Washington, D.C., in 1917, with the Coonleys, continuing in their employ. Over the decades, when the Coonleys embarked for any extended stays at Milfer or Hillside, the Gills were consistently included as part of the entourage. On occasion, they were even invited to enjoy the plays put on by Elizabeth and her friends, in the company of Mr. and Mrs. Coonley.[5] That the Coonleys viewed the Gills as favored employees seems clear. Not only did they build an exquisite cottage for them as part of the integrated estate complex—a very unusual perquisite for Riverside workers of that class—but Mrs. Coonley retained the Gills throughout the Depression, even while other servants were let go.

Another ambiguous point—one which has caused speculation in local sketchy, historic accounts about the resident of the Gardener's Cottage—is Archie's true occupation. He is listed on the 1910 Census as a "Coachman." On the cusp on the Automobile Age, the coachman's job was evolving and included many varied tasks, such as grounds maintenance. Initially, the newlywed Coonleys relied on a loaned coachman. On October 21, 1901, just a few months after their wedding, Queene Ferry wrote to her brother:

Thomas, Mother Coonley's 2nd coachman comes tomorrow with Avery's two horses. Stuart [presumably John Stuart Coonley, Avery's younger brother] and Avery are going to share Thomas between them. We can do it quite easily I think, for our furnace being gas he does not need to do ours early in the a.m. but can get over here in time to clean . . . walks. Louise [Stuart's wife] and I will take every other day with him for window cleaning, rugs, etc.[6]

The "et cetera" in her note suggests that a coachman's scope of work was broadly defined. A little over a year after this note, Archie had apparently been hired into the Coonley estate. Although he'd only been in the U.S. for about a year or two, Archie was considered for a supervisory position with one of the settlement houses with which Avery was involved. Queene Coonley gave insight as to Archie's strong temperament in this note to her brother:

Avery is quite busy with his Settlement business. Did I tell you of a Social Settlement young McCormick [presumably Cyrus Jr.] and Avery & a few others are forming over near the huge McCormick reaper works & the Malleable [Coonley business]? . . . I am not sure that Archie would be equal to keeping a harmonious attitude with the business men. The head resident must be broad enough to see *both* sides.[7]

Given Mr. Coonley's lifelong love of horses and the emergence of the automobile as the newest plaything of the well-to-do, it makes sense that Archie's key responsibility was to handle the horses and maintain the cars. This was a learning experience for all involved. Indeed, in 1911, Mr. Coonley exchanged letters with his brother-in-law Dexter, who, living in Detroit, the center of the automobile world, was an early adopter of the car and offered advice to Avery. Dexter encouraged the avid horseman, Avery, "I am mighty glad you have taken the jump and I do not feel that it means good-bye horses. It simply means good-by utility horses."[8]

Utility or work horses were often used in garden and field-related tasks, such as breaking new ground each spring, and thus they could naturally fall under the domain of the coachman or gardener. Dexter advised leaving the "heavy mechanics for the Packard branch in Chicago" and letting Archie master the gasoline, electricity, oiling, and tires. Avery, a hands-on guy, noted, "I dislike to have anything about the place about which I am not reasonably intelligent. I believe I shall have to learn to run a car."[9] Nonetheless, he planned to convert the estate's chicken coop into a garage, including a pit where Archie could clean the grease from the car and perform simple maintenance.

Archie was invited to Detroit to learn about the newfangled, thirty-horsepower Packard that the Coonleys planned to purchase. A hint of Archie's headstrong personality was revealed while he studied in Detroit. Dexter Ferry reported to Avery: "Archie has a trifle too much confidence in what he can do in a car so that you better watch out a little at first for things happen awfully quick when they do happen and the driver can not for the life of him tell how it happened. You must pick up driving yourself as soon as you can."[10] Attesting to his many skills, Archie's absence from the Riverside estate was felt. Avery noted, "His being away leaves us short-handed not only in the stable but in the house, as we have been depending on his brother and also on Mrs. Gill for some of our work."[11] Needed back home, Archie's trip to Detroit was somewhat curtailed; he learned the basics about the car, and then returned to Riverside.

While his primary forte may have been horses and cars, both Archie and Susan Gill were the proverbial Jack and Jill of all trades. Susan cooked meals while at Milfer, and Archie was known to have performed a multitude of tasks. When the Coonley family stayed at a little lake in Nashotah, Wisconsin, Mrs. Coonley wrote, "We only brought Archie and his wife and they do whatever is necessary & we do the rest." Even though this was a temporary summer place, the Gills and Coonleys maintained a garden, as Queene noted: "This place we have is decidedly rustic and pretty. There are a great many acres but mostly in woods & orchard, so it is little care, there is a good garden, which we had started early in the Spring so we have all our own 'garden truck.'"[12]

Given that Jens Jensen's drawings also refer to Archie's house as the Gardener's Cottage in 1913 (as did Wright's original drawings), and given that Archie was commandeered to perform a wide variety of tasks, it is reasonable to assume that he might have had day-to-day responsibility for the Riverside grounds, assisted by a number of landscape specialists.[13] The gardening field was fertile in Riverside during Archie's time. Many prominent Riverside families had live-in gardeners. The 1910 census shows, for example, that Bessie Sherman, daughter of a founder of Riverside village, employed Englishman Thomas Blair, forty-one, as a gardener. Andrew Johnson, seventy, from Sweden, was a gardener to Village Trustee Robert Sommerville, whose garden in an 1896 photo shows elaborate lawn cutouts of exotic plants. Fellow Swede John Andersen worked in the Munday's gardens, another wealthy Riverside family. These gardeners likely lived in the coach houses of these homes—not nearly as "grand" a dwelling as the Gills' cottage.

Neither a conservatory nor a greenhouse was included in the Coonleys' site plan. There were, however, many options available to Riverside gardeners to secure plants and tools. Of course, Queene Ferry Coonley had direct access to one of the nation's major seedhouses, and correspondence shows that she, on occasion, received seed packages hand-picked by Ferry Seed President and brother, Dexter. Locally, the Schmidt home and greenhouse in Riverside was located on Herbert Road, and other nurseries were nearby. The nationally known Vaughan's seed store, from nearby Western Springs, consistency advertised in Riverside's local paper.[14] The Standard Nursery Company of Rochester, New York, announced shipments of tree stock in the *Riverside News.* Thus, Archie would have had ready access to a variety of plants for the estate. Prior to Jensen's landscape plans, the plant material around the estate was dominated by grapevines hanging from the balconies and by diffident collections of deciduous and evergreen plantings dotting the outlying grounds. Jensen's use of native materials could be had from many nurseries or, in pre-conservation days, from a walk through the woods with a spade and shovel at the right time of the year.

Archie and Susan wove themselves into the fabric of Riverside doings. In July 1915, both were involved in one of the village's earliest major Fourth of July celebrations. Today an established tradition in Riverside, the Fourth of July parade was then fairly new to the village. Although Elizabeth and Queene were out of town, Avery Coonley, as an elected official, had many roles in preparing for the celebration. Joining the festivities, Susan Gill dressed as Columbia and Archie as Uncle Sam.[15] The local paper reported that "Mrs. Archie Gills [sic] of the Villa cottage spent a strenuous Fourth besides riding in the parade in costume, she entertained thirty-three guests at dinner and supper."[16] Presumably, in the absence of Mrs. Coonley, Mrs. Gill was acting as hostess for the estate, known locally as the Villa. One wonders how much of a celebration it was for her preparing meals for thirty-three guests!

Archie and Susan Gill moved with the Coonleys to Washington, D.C., in 1917, renting a house near their Rosedale estate. They remained with the Coonley household, staying with Mrs. Coonley after Avery's death in 1920. During the Depression, Mrs. Coonley, while far from impoverished, did make some economizing moves: renting out the main Rosedale house and making her own quarters in the estate's cottage. In 1932, she wrote to her brother, "Our gardener has gone and 2 more going. I am thinking about Rosedale. I could keep the Gills and live upstairs in my guest house."[17] Once again, Archie might have been pressed into service as the gardener pro tem. The Gills remained with Mrs. Coonley until 1933, when, for reasons unclear, they moved back to Chicago Heights, Illinois. In that year, on October 28, 1933, Susan Gill died unexpectedly. That the Gills were still in good graces with Mrs. Coonley is clear, as her handwritten postscript to her brother Dexter indicates: "Mrs. Gill died in Chicago Saturday. I have only Archie's telegram. Heart trouble carried off 2 sisters in the same sudden way, so I fancy it was that. Poor Archie!" Then, with sisterly attention to family obligations, she adds, "I expect he would think a good deal of a line from you."[18]

Archie remained in Chicago Heights until moving to nearby Crete, Illinois, in about 1941. At some point, he remarried a woman named Nelle. At the age of seventy, Archie died in Crete on December 22, 1947, and he was buried at Acacia Park cemetery in Chicago. Fittingly for Archie the gardener, the sections of this park-like cemetery are named after plants: Azalea, Barberry, Carnation, Magnolia, Maple, Mulberry, Pansy, Primrose, Verbena, and Wistaria. Archie's final resting place is near the Garland, Locust, Poplar, Oak, and Tecoma sections, but it is unmarked. As in life, this gardener preferred anonymity in death, leaving only legacy landscapes to speak for him.[19] But I often think about Archie as I'm working in the garden. What might that headstrong, loyal, hard-working immigrant Englishman think of my third-generation Irish-American family now in his house? Might he roll his eyes at our attempts to restore a native plant garden, and encourage us instead to try the latest David Austin® roses from England? Might he scoff at our use of an "eco-friendly" reel lawn mower and point us toward the labor-saving, gas-powered combustion machines? And what of Susan Gill? Surely, she would appreciate the modern gadgetry in our kitchen. I like to think of Archie and Susan every Fourth of July, as Riverside continues to host its traditional parade. In another time, perhaps, we would have gathered at day's end, on the Gardener's Cottage's front porch, to sip lemonade and listen to the cricket's song fade.

LEAVING THE RIVERSIDE VILLA

THE COONLEYS MOVED to Washington, D.C., in 1917 so Avery could perform his new duties managing publications for the Christian Science Church. Initially, the relocation was thought to be temporary. Almost as an afterthought, Queene Ferry announced the move to her brother with characteristic stoicism and optimism on page five of a six-page, single-spaced, typewritten letter:

> I must tell you of the change in our plans for the winter. Avery has been appointed to the Committee on Publication for the District of Columbia and we shall move to Washington in the next two weeks . . . . It does not seem to me that this move will be a life-long one but we shall probably have to be in Washington for two or three years. We are not disposing of our place here but are in hopes to rent it furnished if the right family turns up . . . . It has been a rather quick move for us but I don't know but quick moves are better than to contemplate things too long in advance.[1]

The Coonleys moved to Rosedale, a centuries-old farmhouse with ten or so acres, in residential Cleveland Park, about five miles northwest of the White House. Unlike their Riverside home, the architecture of the Rosedale house was decidedly traditional, but it satisfied the Coonleys' desire to live amidst natural surroundings.[2] An Associated Press retrospective report noted that Rosedale, at the time of the Coonleys' purchase, ". . . was still really country. There were three horses, two cows, chickens and a farm garden."[3] The 1954 gardener of the estate, Anton Andersen, was quoted, "With its simplicity and natural settings, Rosedale is one of the most beautiful places I've ever seen."[4]

The Riverside estate was left in the able hands of a Mrs. Daniels, who supervised ongoing household affairs. Thornecroft was sold to a Chicago lawyer in 1919. The caretaker cottage at 308 Fairbank was sold to a Mr. Ely, a one-time dry grocer from nearby Lyons, Illinois, who later became a Christian Scientist practitioner—perhaps a Coonley connection.

Finding a single buyer for the estate itself—including the Gardener's Cottage—proved difficult, for the buyer had to have both an appreciation for the architectural work of Frank Lloyd Wright, and the means to maintain it. Since the Coonleys had particular affection for the home, they were reluctant to carve it up, although that would have improved the chances of a sale. As Avery Coonley wrote in 1919, ". . . that house is an important entity to us and has been quite a part of our lives, and a proposal to cut it up is just a little like a proposal to find someone to adopt Elizabeth and to find positions for Mrs. Coonley and myself." [5]

Ads were placed in the Chicago newspapers, as well as in *House Beautiful, Country Life in America,* and other national magazines, to find the right buyer for the entire estate. According to the *Riverside News,* "People came from all parts of the United States to investigate." [6] As the likelihood of preserving the estate intact diminished, the Coonleys began to work with Wright apprentice William Drummond to make needed repairs on the house and to consider alterations, should the estate be divvied up. In the letter exchange between Drummond and Coonley, both Archie's cottage and the Whittlesley stone cottage seemed to be obvious candidates for separate sales. Coonley opined, " . . . it seems to me that even the most important of the small houses you [Drummond] propose would not bring much more than Thornecroft, which we have just sold for $14,000. The others would range from say four or possibly five thousand dollars for Archie's cottage (which would have to have some additional land) up to ten thousand dollars for the next most important." [7] It's unclear how Drummond and Coonley conceived of parceling out the estate or what the "other small houses" were, other than perhaps the playhouse. In addition to Archie's cottage (the Gardener's Cottage) and the stone cottage, their letters refer to a "Central Section" and "Four other sections." Coonley estimated a total sale value of $41,000 for the divided estate, after all necessary alterations and repairs were made.

Thankfully, the estate received its first reprieve when Peter Kroehler, then one of the world's largest furniture manufacturers, purchased the property *in toto*. The timing was both fortuitous and poignant. In October 1919, Queene Coonley's letters to family mentioned that Avery's health was poor; "a difficulty with digestion."[8] Despite some encouraging rallies and a hopeful rest in Tarpon Springs, Florida, Avery Coonley died on April 10, 1920, in Rosedale. In addition to Queene Ferry and Elizabeth, members of the Coonley family were there, and Dexter and Jeannette Ferry had visited shortly before he passed away. Services were attended by "just the family and household," with Lydia Coonley and Blanche Ferry staying on to offer comfort.[9] Adding to Queene Ferry's troubles, the very month that Avery died, a Kroehler contract on the Riverside estate was underway. She prevailed upon her brother, Dexter, to handle the final details. Items, such as outstanding repairs, new curtains, and architectural blueprint ownership, were resolved with Dexter's help, and a new family began life at the Villa.[10] The Kroehlers maintained contact with the Wright office, with correspondence between them outlining various business arrangements around custom furniture.

On at least two later occasions, the Kroehlers approached Wright about selling the house. In 1929, they apparently offered to sell the estate to Wright. He replied:

> I am not yet in a position to buy a home near Chicago, being lucky to have the one that I am already in here in Wisconsin. A year or two from now it looks as though that all might change. I can imagine nothing I could enjoy more than to take over your house and live in it.[11]

The widow Kroehler wrote to Wright in 1951, following Mr. Kroehler's death in August 1950—like the Coonleys before her—asking advice on how to divide up the estate. He wrote:

> I think we can do something to divide the house but it seems a pity. There would be many now I believe willing to pay much more than it cost—if they could buy it. How would you feel about that? I am sure it being in the class of a work of art would be worth much more as unspoiled as possible.[12]

After Avery's death, Queene Ferry Coonley never remarried, but she remained purposeful with her dedication to education and Vassar College. She continued the improvements at Rosedale, an estate quite unlike the Riverside Villa in its traditional architecture and gardens. Dating back to the 1700s, Rosedale had elaborate terraced and formal gardens—a far cry from the naturalistic landscape espoused by Jens Jensen. Yet the intent to marry the landscape to the architecture of the home was a consistent thread between Rosedale and the Coonleys' Riverside estate. Mrs. Coonley commissioned renowned Virginian landscape architect Charles Gillette to help restore Rosedale's landscape to its 1800s roots. Its gardens must have required substantially more maintenance than the Riverside garden. "My grandmother had a team of gardeners starting with a head gardener," recalls Celia Crawford, a Coonley granddaughter.[13]

Ever the progressive thinker, Mrs. Coonley found an opportunity to advance women's rights and to obtain excellent landscaping at Rosedale through her head gardener, Miss Hedwig Krueger, also a Dane (as was Jensen). *The Washington Post* reported:

> Landscape gardening for women is still an almost unknown occupation in America, according to Miss Hedwig Krueger, a charming young Danish girl who has been for some time head-gardener on Mrs. Avery Coonley's estate of eight or nine acres at Cleveland Park. Miss Krueger had studied her profession in both Denmark and Germany, and had, in fact, five years of training before she came to America, so that she may be called a landscape architect . . . Yet, in spite of all this preparation Miss Krueger found it exceedingly difficult to place herself in line for a position as an artistic gardener which might readily have been open to a man . . . she and her brother . . . sought in many cities and in the country a place for her, until, at length Mrs. Avery Coonley heard of the young girl's ambition to become a landscape gardener, and at once employed her.[14]

In the *Washington Post* interview, Krueger gave insight as to how gardens were used at the Coonleys' Rosedale estate and, by inference, at the Riverside Villa: "Here I enjoy providing a kitchen with fresh vegetables . . . . I take care of fruit trees, the lawn and the flowers. It is a great delight to me to beautify the interior of a home with flowers."[15] Queene Ferry Coonley surrounded herself with nature and flowers at all of her residences, including the family vacation home in Milfer and, of course, at Riverside.

Queene Ferry Coonley died at the age of eighty-four on July 10, 1958. Her obituary in *The New York Times* first identified her as a suffragist and then elaborated on her work in progressive education. The last paragraph of the obituary noted that "Mrs. Coonley and her late husband commissioned Frank Lloyd Wright, architect to design a house for them in 1908 . . . Mr. Wright later wrote that the Coonley house was 'one of those I've always regarded with pleasure.'"[16]

After Archie Gill, Gardener

AFTER THE COONLEYS left the Villa at Riverside, what happened to the house and grounds? When Peter and Grace Kroehler bought the property in April 1920, they obtained the main residence, the coachhouse/stables, Stone cottage, and the Gardener's Cottage. Thornecroft had already been sold, as had the Drummond-built caretaker's cottage next to it. Like the Coonleys, the Kroehlers had one child, Kenneth, who lived with them in the large estate.[17] An early issue of the *Riverside News* noted that the Kroehlers had been living for about two years in Riverside's other Frank Lloyd Wright home, the Tomek house, on Nuttall and Bartram roads. The 1920 census for the Kroehlers at this home indicates two servants at the household, neither of whom was a gardener. It is presumed that the Kroehlers retained a come-and-go gardener for their Tomek residence.

An offsite gardener was also employed when the Kroehlers moved into the Coonley estate. Virginia Henry, who lived in the Gardener's Cottage during the Kroehler era, recalls that a gentleman (presumed to be August Taeschler) from the neighboring community of Lyons, Illinois, was the gardener for the estate. Virginia and her parents, Rochelle and Arthur Benwitz, moved into Archie's cottage when the Kroehlers bought it, and they stayed there from 1930 to 1949. Few changes were made to the Gardener's Cottage during this period, although Virginia remembers that the once-open veranda was screened in. Virginia's father was the caretaker and chauffeur for the Kroehler estate, and Virginia has many fond memories of the cottage, the Kroehlers, and Riverside.

Peter Kroehler died in 1950, and the estate was divided. The main residence was bisected into two homes, and the stables and the Gardener's Cottage were sold separately. The teardrop-shaped land parcel was subdivided by developer Arnold Skow, and today it includes five additional homes. Architect Paul Holt and his wife were the first owner/occupants of the Gardener's Cottage, purchasing it directly from Skow about 1952. The Holts enjoyed several decades at the cottage.

Thanks to the efforts of preservationists Carolyn and James Howlett, the estate was spared major remodeling or destruction in the 1950s. The Howletts, who purchased and converted the stables to a residence, raised public awareness of the Coonley estate through articles in *House Beautiful* magazine. The influential magazine reported:

The Coonley house has fared well, so far, having had only 3 owners in 50 years. It is now in the hands of an architect, Arnold Skow, who carefully remodeled its extensive facilities into several dwelling units without spoiling the original concept or beauty. But it may not always fare so well, for we are only just beginning to realize what treasures the recent past contains . . . .[18]

The first major addition was made to the Gardener's Cottage in the 1950s. The Holts built a detached garage and separate driveway between the cottage and the eastern half of the estate's main residence. The two-car garage with a flat roof is architecturally sympathetic to the cottage and estate as a whole. In the 1950s, the Holts also revised the cottage's front entrance and enclosed the screened veranda with windows, making it a year-round space. Notes from previous owners indicate that a low stucco wall separating the Gardener's Cottage from the stables was removed during this timeframe.

In the mid-1960s, the Holts added another 360-square-foot room connecting the garage and the original kitchen. This was the last major alteration to the exterior of the Gardener's Cottage before the estate received National Historic Landmark status in 1970. In the 1990s, the cottage was bought and sold twice by preservation-minded individuals, who made updates and repairs and who started a naturalistic, Jensen-esque garden. Our family has lived in the Gardener's Cottage since March 2004, continuing its ownership by nature-lovers and gardeners.

BE IT EVER SO HUMBLE

THE GARDENER'S COTTAGE lies at the bottom of a small hill on the rounded, northeast corner of the Coonley estate. Originally about 700 square feet, the cottage was a miniature example of the workmanship found in the larger Coonley home. The estate itself, a complex of buildings built between 1907 and 1913 (see page ii), caused Frank Lloyd Wright to reminisce, "I put the best in me into the Coonley house . . . that building was the best I could do then in the way of a house."[1] It was the largest of his implemented Prairie Style homes and the first, according to authors Charles and Berdeana Aguar, to use his "zoned plan," based on the Japanese *sukiya* building style.[2] This Zen-inspired architecture emphasizes harmony with nature and interrelated but distinct spaces for household activities. The original plan for the estate included the main residence, servants' quarters, garage and stables, and the gardener's house, all clustered together on the same parcel of land amidst courtyard gardens.

The Coonleys acquired the Whittlesley stone cottage, the only other house on that parcel, for use as a "cottage school" for daughter Elizabeth and her friends. They commissioned Wright's apprentice William Drummond to build Thornecroft for their cottage schoolteachers and an ancillary caretaker's cottage, diagonally across from the Gardener's Cottage. Still later, Wright designed a separate playhouse (which Mrs. Coonley called the Workshops) for their daughter, Elizabeth.[3]

Deservedly so, of the Wright-designed buildings, the main Coonley residence and playhouse typically receive the most scholarly and public

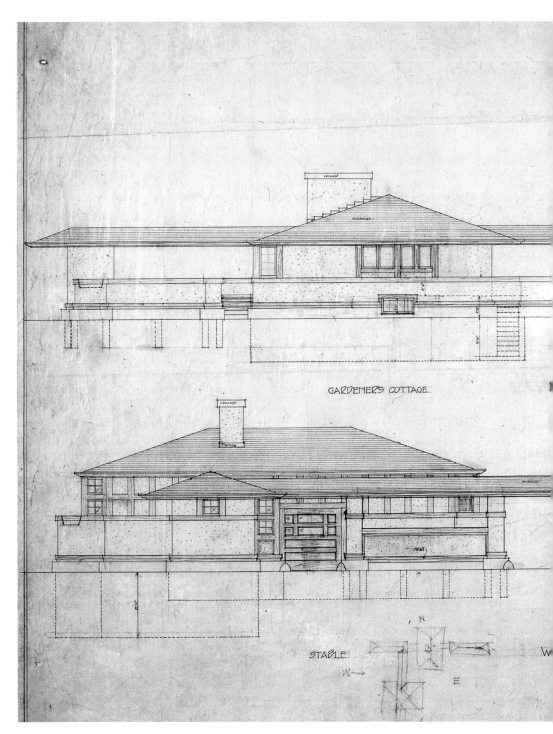

GARDENER'S COTTAGE

STABLE

Frank Lloyd Wright's elevations for the Gardener's Cottage (upper left and lower right).
Note the connecting roof (now removed) and adjacent stables.

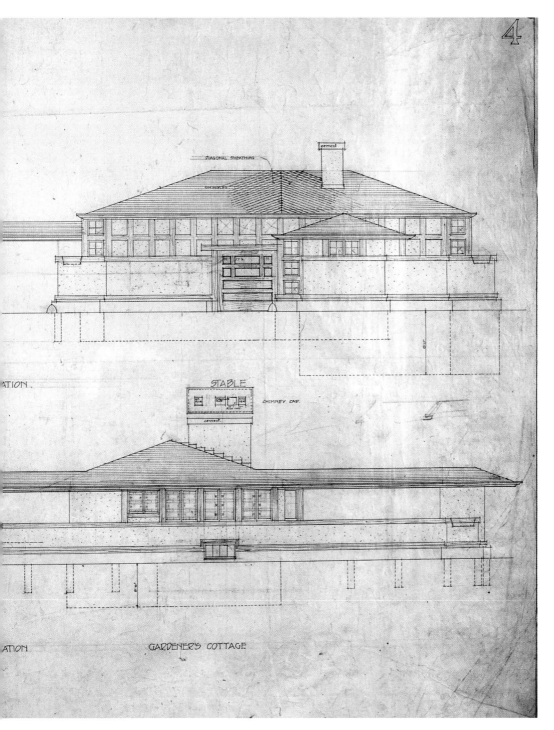

4

DIAGONAL SHEATHING

cement

SHINGLES

ATION

STABLE

CHIMNEY CAP.

cement

ATION

GARDENER'S COTTAGE

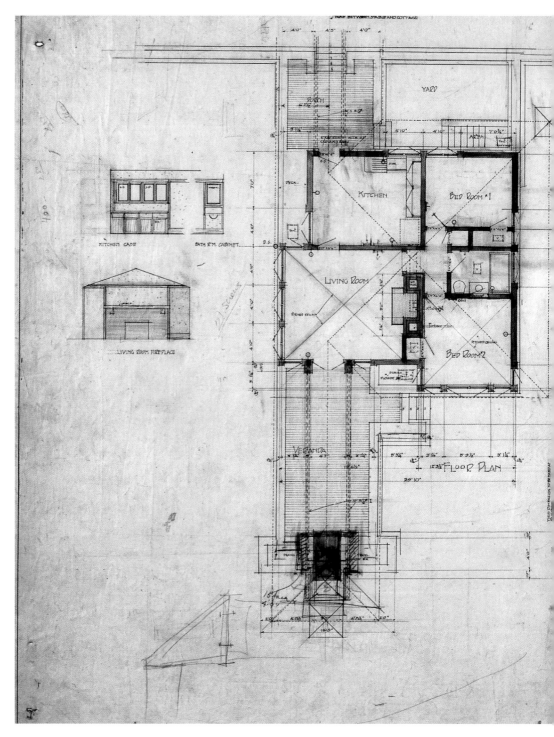

Frank Lloyd Wright's plan view of the Gardener's Cottage, including details of the kitchen cabinetry and hearth.

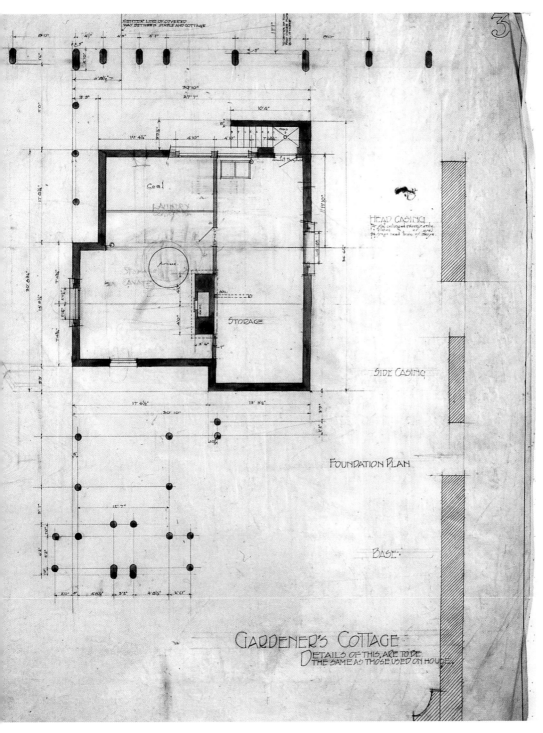

CENTER LINE OF COVERED
WAY BETWEEN STABLE AND COTTAGE

Coal

LAUNDRY

Furnace

STORAGE

HEAD CASING

SIDE CASING

FOUNDATION PLAN

BASE

GARDENER'S COTTAGE
DETAILS OF THIS ARE TO BE
THE SAME AS THOSE USED ON HOUSE.

attention. In the main residence, the windows, views, woodwork, murals, and Wright's pioneering sculpture of interior and exterior space are breathtaking. The playhouse enchants not only for its fanciful windows and delightful views of forest and river, but also the notion that a full-sized house was built strictly for children. Even the stables have received critical acclaim, largely for the sensitive conversion to a home.[4]

Overlooked by most scholars (but not by curious passersby) is the modest Gardener's Cottage. Of all the grander buildings, it is the only one which continues to serve its original purpose today—that of a single-family home. Whereas the stables and playhouse were converted to homes and the main residence itself was bisected to accommodate two separate owners, the Gardener's Cottage has, through its history, always housed a small family. The grounds of the Gardener's Cottage, too, remain, both in scale and intent, true to their original design. Since the Coonley parcel was subdivided in the 1950s, the long west and southwesterly views from the main residence have been compromised. The sunken garden, integral to the unified design of the complex interior grounds, has been significantly altered, and elements now belong to multiple owners. The playhouse, formerly tucked into the woods, is currently one of many houses in the nearby parcel of Coonley land, now subdivided. All of these repurposed structures are exquisite, and their owners rightfully enjoy accolades for their high-quality restoration efforts. Yet, oddly, the simple Gardener's Cottage seems to impart a more visceral sense of history. There are no new homes built contiguous to its grounds, and it remains in context next to a wing of the main residence and the stables. Its main views—across one of Olmsted's green triangles and over to Thornecroft—have not changed. Certainly, the Gardener's Cottage has been remodeled over time. The most obvious changes—enclosing the open-air porch and adding a garage and bedroom—occurred in the 1950s, before the estate achieved National Historic Landmark status in 1970. But the relationship between home and immediate grounds has not been drastically altered—a rarity among Wright buildings.

As noted on Wright's plan of the cottage where "details of this are to be the same as those used on house," the architecture of the Gardener's Cottage blends seamlessly with that of the larger estate. Clearly, its size and interior finishes are much more humble. It is not Wright's first diminutive family home, but it is the first to replicate, on a small scale, the sumptuous architecture of a large estate.[5] The bands of windows, cedar-trimmed walls, clay tile roof, gutter system, and stucco echo that of the main estate, but interior finishes are of simpler materials, such as Douglas-fir and pine.

The siting of the Gardener's Cottage is also one of Wright's greatest gifts to its occupants. With mostly east, south, southeast, and southwest exposures, the cottage captures sunlight in all seasons. From the prow-shaped front porch (now enclosed), one of Olmsted's triangular green spaces frames the long view to the grassy park and Des Plaines River and extends across the borrowed landscape. What a luxury this porch must have been to the gardener! Nestled down into the base of the hill, the cottage's porch channels cooling southwest breezes and refreshing glimpses of sparkling river.

The porch, or veranda per Wright's plan, is a long, narrow room (about eleven by twenty-two feet), reaching to within eight feet of the sidewalk. Virginia Henry recalls that, during her tenure living in the Gardener's Cottage, the porch was screened in.[6] She remembers the French doors, leading to the living room, as being the main front entrance to the home. Wright's plan shows a built-in flower box hugging the home at the front entrance, visible through windows from the original front bedroom.[7]

From the French doors one enters directly into the living room. The centerpiece of the room is a large hearth, built of ochre brick and trimmed with a substantial mantel of pine. The fireplace trim and wood molding around the room is of Douglas-fir and pine, and they display Wright's workingman's version of ornamentation. With the room's pyramidal pitched ceiling, the hearth forms its own home-within-a-home. Beautifully mellowed 2¼-inch pine flooring glows throughout this and all of the original rooms in the home. The living room, while only fourteen by fourteen feet, seems more spacious with its southwest-facing windows and pyramidal ceiling, one of two such ceilings in the house. The windows are ample—each with a simplified L-shaped design of three iridescent, green-glass squares. It must originally have been even more light-filled; Virginia Henry theorizes that two windows were removed during the remodeling in the 1950s. By enclosing the veranda in this remodel, light that once streamed through the front doors would have been lost.[8] Henry also recalls a large radiator in the corner near the fireplace. Since Wright is said to have abhorred exposed radiators, it is curious how this came about.

The living room opens directly into the kitchen. Old hinge marks indicate that a door once separated the rooms. The kitchen, updated to twenty-first century technology, is about the same size as the original floor plan and retains the original flooring. Windows were evidently relocated, and two south- and west-facing ones were removed within the 1950s addition of a bedroom.[9] Wright's sketch shows details for both kitchen and bath cabinetry—spare rectangular units with raised or inset panels. Virginia Henry's hand-drawn layout of the kitchen, circa the 1940s, confirms the implementation of Wright's drawing and shows the cabinets and cooking range lining one wall only (instead of the current U-shaped arrangement of cabinets), suggesting less storage and, perhaps, more room for an eat-in kitchen.

On Wright's plan, windows in the kitchen and living room open to a small, outdoor deck (now a closet in the remodeled addition). West of the deck and the house was a connecting tile-roofed pergola between the stables and the Gardener's Cottage. A gravel-paved alley, or service lane, separated these two buildings and led to the street on the north, now Coonley Road. A little yard was indicated northeast of the pergola that included exposed stairs to the basement of the Gardener's Cottage.

The Gardener's Cottage has a below-ground basement, once accessible by exterior stairs but now enclosed. Wright purportedly disliked basements—dismissing them as clammy, moldy spaces—and he did not provide for them in the main Coonley estate. Perhaps the location of the cottage at the base of the hill, or a need for workspace for the gardener, dictated this feature. Wright designed a full basement under the entire house, with a crawlspace under the porch. One area was for the furnace, laundry, and receipt of coal; the other, with a dirt floor, was specified for storage. Above-ground windows keep the space well-lit. Virginia Henry recalled a fruit cellar in the basement—a seven-by-five-foot enclosure near the basement door. For the gardener, perhaps this fruit cellar and space to wash up after a day's hard labor were needed.

Back on the main level, two bedrooms complete the original house on its east side. The back children's bedroom once had closets near the east window, per Virginia Henry's layout and also on Wright's sketch. Interestingly, one of Wright's windows opened into the closet. A bath with a clawfoot tub, per Henry's recollection, lay between the children's bedroom and the front bedroom. This room, presumably the parent's room, has a band of leaded-glass windows that wraps around the corner. The room had one closet (now two with the remodeling) and a pyramidal ceiling. Here lies a key difference in Wright's design for the workingman: whereas second-floor windows afforded privacy to his well-to-do clients, the windows in the single-floor Gardener's Cottage bedroom are plainly visible from the street. Early photographs show privacy shades (with open-work squares matching the window's glass pattern) screening the front bedroom.

Besides enclosing the front porch, a new wing was added to the Gardener's Cottage in the 1960s. This wing, extending southwest from the kitchen and living room, includes a bedroom, full bath, and garage. The addition is built on a concrete slab and has a flat roof. Subsequent owners applied for, and received, permission from the local historical preservation committee to change the addition's front windows to match the cottage's original leaded-glass windows. Purists may argue against any additions to a Frank Lloyd Wright house, even though the architect himself often remodeled his creations. This addition makes the home suitable for today's living—where a gardener might actually have an automobile.

The materials used and physical orientation of the Gardener's Cottage were meant to complement the main estate but unquestionably befit the cottage in its own right. As a single-story structure, the cottage blends beautifully with its natural surroundings—nature is that much closer than in Wright's two-story Prairie School homes. To marry the home with nature, Wright specified a number of "box-breaking" windows that wrapped around the corners of the rooms. He detailed a unique window design for the cottage, harmonizing with the simple elegance of the structure itself. The design is symmetrical across two casement windows. In some instances—for example, in the front bedroom, which has a row of four windows—a matched pair of single-casement windows offset the middle set of double windows, thus retaining the overall sense of symmetry. Today, although some windows have been removed, the views from all rooms capture Olmsted's green spaces and a Jensen-esque garden—truly blending the outdoors and indoors. For gardeners of yesterday and today, it is the best of both worlds.

The seductive real estate advertisement that initially lured us to the Gardener's Cottage promised not only "a small masterpiece," but also a "small house that lives large." Although its original footprint was expanded by additions in the 1950s and 1960s, the cottage would not do for a very large family. As my husband, Mike, says, "You really have to like each other to live here." Yet, of all the Riverside homes in which I've lived—all with greater square footage—the Gardener's Cottage feels the most expansive. Frank Lloyd Wright packaged the whole outdoors—sunlight and natural views—in the organic architecture of this cozy, compact cottage.

In the lower right of this photograph by Jens Jensen, ca. 1913, the southeast corner of the Gardener's Cottage roof is visible. The gravel service drive between the Gardener's Cottage and the main estate was removed with the cottage's remodeling. Courtesy of the Archives of the Sterling Morton Library at The Morton Arboretum, Lisle, Illinois.

The remodeled Gardener's Cottage includes a garage where the gravel service drive once existed. Photo by the author, 2005.

Note the low wall (no longer extant) separating the Gardener's Cottage from the stables (at right) in this ca. 1912 postcard of the Coonley estate. From the author's collection.

Jens Jensen took this photograph, ca. 1913, of the existing plantings near the Gardener's Cottage before he redesigned the estate's grounds. Courtesy of the Archives of the Sterling Morton Library at The Morton Arboretum, Lisle, Illinois.

In summer, thickets of shrubs surrounded the Gardener's Cottage, though they were not part of Jensen's plan. Photo, ca. 1930, courtesy of Virginia Henry.

The open veranda offered cooling breezes in the fall. Note the window curtains needed for privacy, but they were not specified by Wright. Photo, ca. 1930, courtesy of Virginia Henry.

During the Kroehler era, the veranda was screened in.
Photo, ca. 1935, courtesy of Virgina Henry.

Today, the veranda is a four-season room. The two matching chairs
are from the Kroehler Manufacturing Co., whose namesake was the
second owner of the Coonley estate. The ceiling mural, by Jennifer
Holman, depicts plants favored by Jens Jensen: Rosa setigera,
hawthorn, and crabapple branches. Photo by the author, 2005.

This photograph of the front entryway, ca. 1935, shows the half-wall that no longer exists. Courtesy of Virginia Henry.

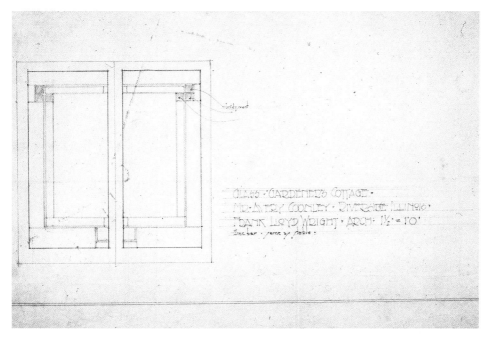

Frank Lloyd Wright's sketch of the Gardener's Cottage window detail. Image © The Frank Lloyd Wright Foundation, Arizona/Art Resource, New York.

View to the exterior from the original main bedroom. Photo by the author, 2005.

View to the exterior from the guest room. Photo by the author, 2005.

Left: View to the south from the cottage prow. Right: View to the north from the cottage prow.
Photos by the author, 2005.

Present-day view of the hearth, showing the original pine mantel and horizontal brick.
Photo by the author, 2005.

View to the exterior from the hearth room. Photo by the author, 2005.

The present-day view of the east wall of the Gardener's Cottage is essentially the same as shown in Wright's plan (see page 44, upper left). Photo by the author, 2005.

Frank Lloyd Wright's Small Homes and Cottages

FRANK LLOYD WRIGHT'S Usonian homes, initially built during the Depression to address his perceived need for elegant homes on a working man's budget, receive critical acclaim as small-scale masterpieces. But, long before the 1930s, Wright was interested in low-cost, artful homes. In July 1901, the *Ladies Home Journal* published Wright's article and design for "A Small House with 'Lots of Room in It.'" The two-story, four-bedroom house had about 2,000 square feet, not counting the basement, closets, and pantries. Wright estimated that the home would cost about $5,835.

The Gardener's Cottage on the Coonley estate is, arguably, Wright's first example of a small-scale, permanent home built with his signature attention to siting and detail. At about 700 square feet (without the porch), the Gardener's Cottage was significantly smaller than the prototype featured in the *Ladies Home Journal*, yet it was eminently livable. Ironically, if it had been sold separately in 1919 after the Coonleys moved, its estimated sales price ranged between $4,000 and $6,000, about the price tag Wright estimated for the prototype.

Some earlier Wright homes have been called cottages, but that is a relative term in Victorian era architecture. Wright remodeled the Heurtley cottage, for example, in 1902 in Marquette Island, Michigan. Although built as a summer home, it is a multi-story structure quite in keeping with an upscale summer retreat. Other Wright-designed summer cottages predate the Coonley Gardener's Cottage. He built a summer residence for his mentor, architect Louis Sullivan, and a guest house and home for client, James Charnley, in Ocean Springs, Mississippi, in 1890 (the latter terribly damaged in August 2005 by Hurricane Katrina). The two-story Robert Lamp Cottage, also a summer home, was built in 1893 in Wisconsin. George Gerts's Bridge Cottage (1902, Michigan) was a multi-story affair with two fireplaces. Wright also designed cottages for the speculative Como Orchard Summer Colony in Montana (1908) and sundry other summer homes that, in the parlance of the day, were termed cottages. But these examples, unlike the Gardener's Cottage, were initially built for seasonal or part-time living, often for wealthy clients, and they were generally much larger than what we would call a cottage today.

Prior to the Coonley estate, Wright built two cottages for the working person, as part of larger estates. The Ward W. Willits Gardener's Cottage with Stables (1901, Highland Park, Illinois) is a two-

Olmsted's green triangular parkway can be viewed from the Gardener's Cottage prow room. Photo by the author, 2009.

story, stucco home integrated with the stables. This cottage, while similar in style to the main residence, is located behind it, much like many coach houses of Victorian days. To approach the home, one would need to pass by the main residence—its siting clearly marked it as a dependency outbuilding. Fully connected with the stables, the Willits's gardener's quarters were above the carriage house, next to the hay loft—hardly the "sumptuous" quarters afforded to Archie and Susan Gill. The Darwin Martin Gardener's Cottage (1905, Buffalo, New York) was added piecemeal after the multi-building estate was built. A lovely two-story structure, it is built of stucco and does not match the brick of the main estate.

The Coonley Gardener's Cottage is unique in that it was built as a stand-alone, single-family residence for the working person, featuring exterior details matching a grand estate and its own private entrance. Furthermore, it is brilliantly sited not only to balance the overall estate composition, but also to capture its own exquisite views provided through Olmsted's landscape plan for Riverside. Enhanced by Jens Jensen's landscape design that was tailored to the scale of this house, the Gardener's Cottage is not an appendage or afterthought to the main residence; it is an elegant home of its own right, whose original purpose as a small-scale family residence has endured throughout the decades.

A LANDSCAPE LEGACY

DURING HIS SCOUTING mission for the Riverside Improvement Company in 1868, Frederick Law Olmsted noted great potential in Riverside's natural features. His full plan for Riverside was never realized, due to the project's financial troubles. Portions of the village, therefore, remained undeveloped in the thirty to forty years before the Coonleys arrived. When the Coonleys chose Block 2 in Riverside's First Division as the site of their new home, it was a "rather unsightly spot," according to one local account.[1] Perhaps this referred to the unimproved state of the land— covered with the very native plants that Jens Jensen would later celebrate. Riverside had always been a popular destination for nature lovers. For peak crabapple and hawthorn blooms, Riverside was the first stop on the Suburban Railroad's "Wildflower Route," and it also received top billing on many recommended hikes. Rich and poor alike visited Riverside in the first series of five walks sponsored by the Playground Association of Chicago in 1908 (which evolved into Jens Jensen's Prairie Club).

Records dating back to 1871, just a few years after Olmsted and Vaux's General Plan for Riverside, show that important plant hunters, such as H. H. Babcock, frequented Riverside to collect specimens. During the time that the Coonleys lived in Riverside, plant collectors found wild plants from spring through fall. In spring, there were Cow parsnip (*Heracleum maximum*), Dutchman's breeches (*Dicentra cucullaria*), Prairie alum root (*Heuchera richardsonii*), red trillium (*Trillium recurvatum*), Starry false Solomon's seal (*Maianthemum stallatum*), wild hyacinth

(*Camassia scilloides*), and violet (*Viola.*). In summer, collectors found meadow anemone (*A. canadense*), moneywort (*Lysimachia nummularia*), stiff arrowhead (*Sagittaria rigida*), swamp verbena (*Verbena hastate*), and wild gooseberry (*Ribes missouriense*). Late summer and early fall produced American bellflower (*Campanula Americana*), crested sedge (*Carex cristatella*), obedient plant (*Physostegia virginiana*), purple giant hyssop (*Agastache scrophulariifolia*), and Eared false foxglove (*Tomanthera auriculata*)—now an Illinois threatened species.[2]

Much of this natural beauty could be found along the Des Plaines River and its woods, which outlined the promontory that was to become the Coonley estate. Wright's architecture aimed to complement these natural surroundings, as did Jensen's landscape designs. Before Jensen's input, circa 1913, Wright's landscaping contributions were concentrated in dense planting areas adjacent to the house. His signature grapevines draped from built-in planter boxes that framed the main estate's windows. Within the controlled privacy of enclosed courtyards, Wright provided a large, sunken garden north of the stables, a raised planting space between the Gardener's Cottage and stables, and, north of the trellis, a raised sitting garden with built-in curved benches and tables.

Jensen took photographs and a site inventory as part of his design process. His topographical map, dated January 1912, shows more than 300 existing trees or shrub groupings on the property, the vast majority oaks. Jensen's planting plan, dated October 1913, carves adventure out of the scattered, amorphous woods and adds intrigue to Wright's regimented gardens. Jensen offered alternating sun openings with naturalistic groves of native trees and shrubs, and he interspersed evocative paths, such as the "white clover trail," among the massed plant groupings. The entire perimeter of the teardrop-shaped parcel was to be bordered with an understory of native shrubs and trees, particularly crabapple and sumac. Accents of dogwood, hawthorn, highbush cranberry, native plums, redbuds, and witch hazel are also introduced in the outer border. The border is drawn irregularly, suggesting not an impenetrable fortress but an inviting thicket that mirrors the tangled riverbank below.

In the sunken garden, Jensen's plan featured a cruciform-shaped planting bed, with a cross of white clover outlined by L-shaped beds of flowers. A small, rectangular pool lies to the east, with a rose-covered trellis serving as backdrop. This cruciform design may have predated Jensen, although early plans by Wright show

One of Jensen's sunlit openings creates a "clearing" amidst the brilliance of autumn foliage in the northeast section of the cottage's garden. Photo by the author, 2005.

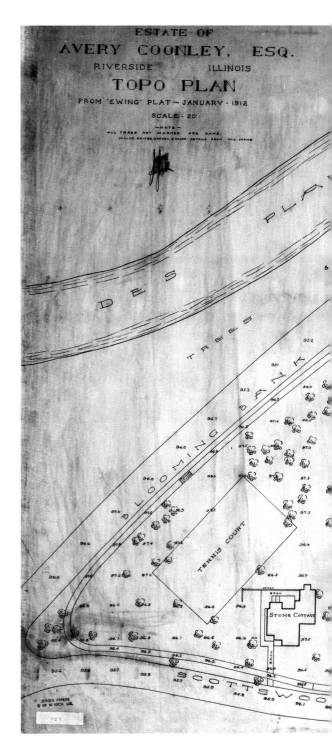

Jensen's topographic plan (1912) documented the many existing mature oaks and other native trees and shrubs. The Gardener's Cottage appears in the lower right of the plan. Jens Jensen Collection, Bentley Historical Library, University of Michigan.

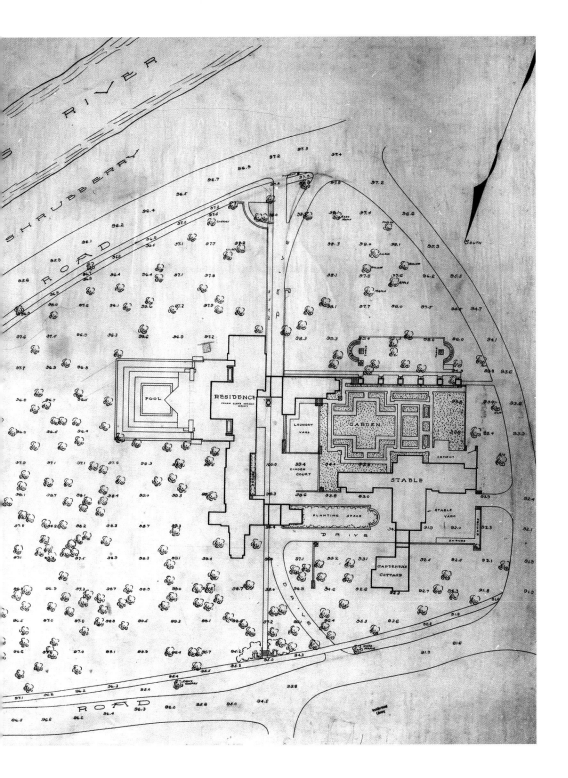

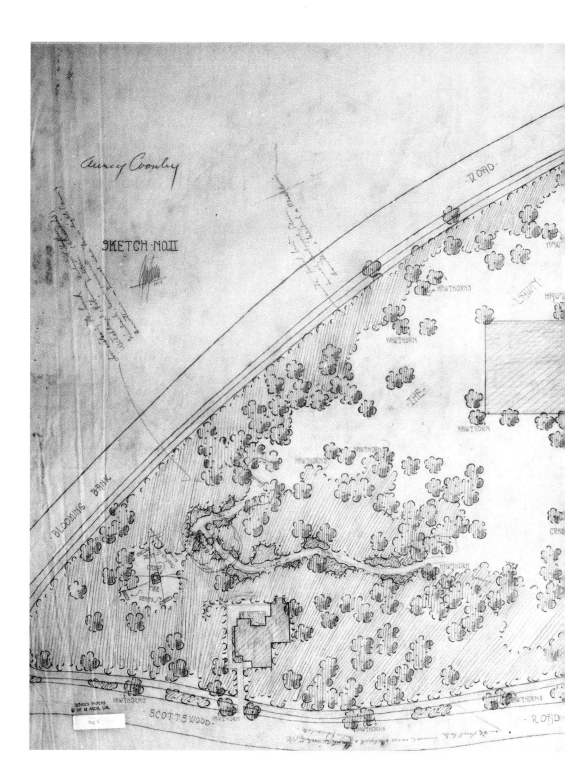

Avery Coonley

SKETCH NO II

ROAD

HAWTHORNS

HAWTHORN

THE

BLOOMING BANK

HAWTHORNS

HAWTHORN

HAWTHORNS

HAWTHORN

CREEK

HAWTHORNS

SCOTTSWOOD

HAWTHORN

HAWTHORNS

ROAD

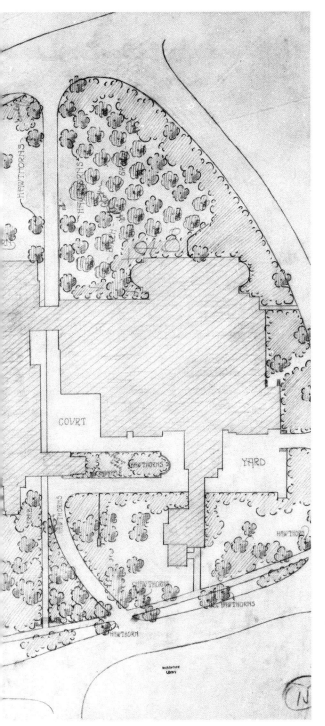

HAWTHORNS

HAWTHORNS

HAWTHORN

COURT

HAWTHORNS

YARD

HAWTHORN

HAWTHORNS

HAWTHORN

HAWTHORNS

HAWTHORN

Architecture Library

N

Jens Jensen's conceptual sketch, ca. 1913, for the Coonley estate shows shrub and tree massings and open clearings. The Gardener's Cottage is located in the lower right of this drawing. Notice the clearings on either side of the cottage and the rectilinear service drive behind it. Jens Jensen Collection, Bentley Historical Library, University of Michigan.

interlocking squares. Jensen modified the raised sitting garden that so offended him with strategically placed hawthorns that afforded privacy to each seating group. Working counterclockwise from the sitting garden, Jensen designed a fairly dense birch grove at the far northwest corner of the property. This contrasted nicely with the open space of "The Lawn" on the western side of the driveway. At the driveway entrance, and at the beginning of the main residence, he placed foursomes of hawthorns. Small clusters of hawthorn are the only trees positioned sparingly near the rest of home—presumably so as to avoid smothering Wright's architectural masterpiece. The only other house-related plantings Jensen specified was indicated on a note on the planting plan: "*ampelopsis veitchii* on all walls." Presumably, this Boston ivy, while not native, would provide excellent summer greenery and autumn color.

The lawn opens into an even wider space, identified as the clearing, which wraps around the southwestern side of the house, a fit setting around a jewel. The views from second-floor windows of the main estate, and from the dramatic reflecting pool, thus progressed from the smooth lawn to captivating woodlands, to the Des Plaines River beyond. A campfire circle, an interpretation of Jensen's trademark council rings—circular outdoor seating areas intended to promote a sense of fellowship, community, and democracy—replaced an awkward tennis court seen on Wright's drawings, about two-thirds of the way from the residence to the promontory point. The campfire, like Jensen's council rings, was sequestered in the woodland of crabapple, hawthorns, nine-bark, and redbuds, and it reached through the "white clover trail." Continuing counterclockwise from the campfire, various minor clearings are interspersed among clusters of native plantings. Jensen extended the landscape out into the public parkway with groupings of crabapples, hawthorns, and plums.

Pre-Jensen views of the landscape around the Gardener's Cottage show an uninspired row of deciduous shrubs aligned with Prussian precision along the perimeter of the property. Between the Gardener's Cottage and stables, Wright had specified a low wall.[3] The march of the deciduous shrubs extended along this wall. A few specimen plantings of (seemingly) white pine trees interrupt the monotony.

Jensen's proposed landscaping around the Gardener's Cottage broke the shrub brigade with curves and naturalistic groupings of native trees. Plantings were fairly dense, perhaps affording the gardener some privacy that was lacking in the home's first-floor windows and proximity to the sidewalk. From his living room windows, the gardener could look southwest to an open area with clusters of raspberry bushes; appropriately, only the landscaping around the Gardener's Cottage specifies edible fruits, such as raspberries and blackberries. From the kitchen window, crabapple trees framed the gravel service drive. Beyond that, the raised planting area between the cottage and stables was planted with hawthorn, *Rosa setigera,* and crabapples— beautiful from both ground level at the cottage and looking down from the bed- rooms of the main residence. The service drive behind the Gardener's Cottage was also lined with blackberry bushes on the south and with roses and sumac on the north.

Roses also were nestled near the foundation of the Gardener's Cottage on the northeast, and *Rosa blanda* encompassed the sidewalk leading to the front door. Surely, their perfume would have delighted the gardener and his family as they relaxed on the front porch after a long, hard day. The southwestern corner of the porch was shaded by a hawthorn tree, which provided privacy and shade when leafed out in summer months. Like the rest of the grounds, the perimeter of land surrounding the Gardener's Cottage was framed by a naturalistic planting of crabapples, hawthorns, and *Rosa setigera.*

Today, little of the original landscape remains around the Gardener's Cottage. A venerable oak anchors the northeast point of the property, as it has for more than 200 years. An old apple tree still produces fruit at the base of the driveway; it cannot be 100 years old, of course, but it is perhaps a scion from one of the teaching trees planted for little Elizabeth Coonley. But, thanks to the collaborative efforts of several recent owners and help from experts on Prairie School landscape architecture, the Gardener's Cottage blooms with native prairie and woodland plants—just as Jens Jensen had in mind.

On the western side of the house, between the driveway and enclosed porch, a prairie garden soaks up the sun. Native plants—including cardinal flower, compass plant, coneflowers, goldenrod, milkweed, and spiderwort—bloom in unbridled profusion. Their long, prairie plant roots anchor the soil—a useful attribute since there is a gentle slope from the driveway to the porch. In front of the cottage, a colorful collage of bird-friendly flowers and shrubs bloom. Framing the front door, a rain garden, designed to recycle efficiently stormwater runoff, flows from a Jensen- esque stone bird pool. To the east, informal borders layered with native trees and shrubs curve gracefully around an open clearing of lawn. Blessed with the visionary legacy of three American artists—Olmsted, Wright, and Jensen—the cottage's gardens today embrace Jensen's naturalistic spirit and enhance both Wright's cottage and Olmsted's village.

As stewards of the Gardener's Cottage, it is somewhat intimidating to design and maintain the grounds and landscape. Everyone has an opinion, and, since it is part of a National Historic Landmark, the grounds of the Gardener's Cottage are constantly on view.

Our family has benefited from many experts. Mary Ann and John Crayton, previous owners, began a beautiful native plant garden. Scott Mehaffey, then the Morton Arboretum's landscape architect, designed the garden beds and trees and shrubs. When we moved in, we took the first year to get acquainted with the plants. By the second year, I could identify most of them. By the third year, as native plants will do, we were nearly overgrown. (Thankfully, I drew on the expertise of Kurt Dreisilker, the Morton Arboretum's Manager of Natural Resources, to teach me how to prune properly all the woody plants.) Then, neighboring construction caused a pipeline to run directly through the focal point of the garden. A major tree was lost, and hundreds of natural perennials perished.

We took the opportunity to consider ways of making a native garden more intuitive and familiar to passersby. Borrowing from the success of Chicago's Lurie Garden in Millennium Park, we added some subtle cultivars to the native mix. We asked Roy Diblik, of Northwind Perennial Farms, for advice. Diblik, who translated into Midwestern plants many of Piet Oudolf's specifications for the Lurie Garden, grew the plants at Northwind. He gave me the courage to remove native plants that were "thugs," or aggressive growers. We like the result: a Jensen-inspired garden with mostly natives and a few popular cultivars for accents. With hundreds of species in the garden, there is something for everyone.

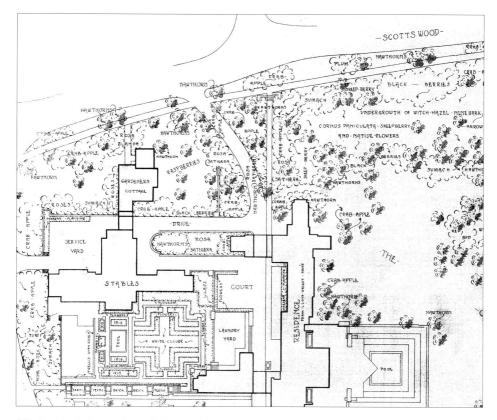

The Gardener's Cottage (upper left), according to Jensen's planting plan circa
1913, was to be surrounded by crabapples, hawthorns, sumac, and raspberries.
Jens Jensen Collection, Bentley Historical Library, University of Michigan.

Wildlife are attracted to the cottage's gardens, even in winter. Photo by the author, 2009.

Southwest of the Gardener's Cottage prow room, a naturalistic prairie garden grows several feet tall. Photo by the author, 2005.

Native coneflowers adorn the entrance to the Gardener's Cottage.
Photo by the author, 2005.

The entryway, remodeled ca. 1955, is framed and softened by trees and shrubs. Photo by the author, 2005.

A Jensen-inspired bird pool at the Gardener's Cottage collects groundwater and recycles it in an environmentally friendly rain garden. Photo by Alexa Rubenstein, 2009.

Jens Jensen, Landscape Architect

JENS JENSEN (1860–1951) grew up surrounded by the vast fields of his family's ancestral farm in Denmark. These scenes and views of the nearby North Sea inspired him to love the endless, flat plains surrounding his adopted homeland in Chicago. Arriving there in 1886, Jensen found work in Chicago's west parks, advancing from a laborer to superintendent. His "American Garden," designed for a corner of Union Park in 1888, was warmly embraced by the public, which enjoyed the display of humble, native plants. This use of native plantings bucked the trendy Victorian-era love of exotic varieties, and it became a design trademark for Jensen, along with naturalistic groupings of plant materials, clearings (or sun openings) amidst woodlands, stratified stonework, and council rings.

Jensen was a charismatic, principled, and strongly opinionated individual who gained regional and national prominence as a landscape architect, especially during the early twentieth century. Refusing to participate in the corrupt politics of Chicago's west parks, Jensen began his private practice in the early 1900s. His client base included some of the wealthiest individuals in Chicago and the nation: the Armours, Henry Ford and Edsel B. Ford, the Insulls, McCormicks, Rosenwalds, Ryersons, and Swifts all commissioned Jensen to design their private estates. After a change in management, Jensen also resumed work for the Chicago Parks, creating both small neighborhood parks and the larger parks on the West Side. While largely concentrated in the Midwest, Jensen's work extended from Maine to California. In the 1930s, Jensen moved to his erstwhile summer home in Ellison Bay, in Door County, Wisconsin, establishing The Clearing, a "school of the soil" for aspiring landscape architects that continues to this day.

Jensen was passionately committed to the preservation and reintroduction of natural areas in and around Chicago. He either founded or cofounded a number of early conservation groups, including the Friends of Our Native Landscape and the Prairie Club. These groups explored Chicago's outlying natural areas and helped to preserve much of today's green space. Like Frederick Law Olmsted, Jensen believed that naturalistic landscaping would have positive effects on society. Jensen's designs, while decades younger and stylistically unique, are very much at home in Olmsted's Riverside.

Tall, mature trees frame the Gardener's Cottage, as seen from Thornecroft. Photo, ca. 1935, courtesy of Virginia Henry.

LIVING IN THE GARDENER'S COTTAGE

ONE MORNING, SHORTLY after our family moved in the Gardener's Cottage, I sat down with a cup of coffee in a wooden rocking chair on the veranda. Windows framed a view across our tiny Jens Jensen-inspired garden, past Olmsted's triangle of greenery, down to the Des Plaines River. With trees just budding out and with heavy spring rains, the river was high and sparkling. It seemed to me that Archie and Susan Gill must have sat just like this, enjoying the view. Of course, there were differences: walls had been added to the veranda, which, from this vantage point, happily screened out later-built homes. I also doubted that the gardener and his wife would have had time for a leisurely cup of coffee in the morning. More likely, they sat there after the day's work was done, enjoying soft evening breezes and the sound of the crickets and birdsong.

The purity and longevity of Frank Lloyd Wright's design for this simple home continues to amaze us. Exquisitely sited to maximize the sun, the house absorbs the best of nature's beauty, from sunrise to sundown, year-round. At dawn, sunlight brightens our son's bedroom, nudging him gently from sleep. Later in the morning, our office is fully illuminated into a cheerful workplace. As daylight gathers force, the cottage's main living spaces—the veranda and living room—capture the sun's rays. In the living room, shadows from Wright's elegantly simple, leaded-glass windows stretch and bend across the pitched ceiling, as they have for the past century. Tall plants outside—Queen of the Prairie, milkweed, and coneflowers—cast their own silhouettes in late summer, and a prairie plant puppet show dances across our fireplace mantel.

A friend asked reasonably upon our moving in, "When are you going to cut all those weeds down?" Little did he know that a key reason we bought the house was for the "weeds." As a veteran gardener, it was humbling to struggle to identify many of the native plants surrounding the cottage. Some quickly came back to me—the shooting stars and prairie roses gathered by the fistful as a child; sumac, redbuds, and oaks, which once filled Chicago's forest preserves. Others I had to study and key to plant guides—natives once prevalent but now found only in choice nurseries. I made labels for many and continue to identify and add more, both for ourselves and passersby. The flowers and grasses struggle to escape their gently curved beds, a celebration of Midwestern woods and prairie. It is a garden different from the many smooth lawns in Riverside, but, because our corner location is unfettered by adjoining yards, this environmentally friendly space has its own aesthetic. The garden is a favorite destination for wildlife. Some argue that Olmsted wanted only identical, democratic lawns in his suburbs, but I look at the efforts he took to preserve native plants, both in Riverside and on his famed Wooded Island in Chicago, and I think he would approve.

As the day wanes, the sun sets behind the cottage, leaving a sky of pinks, purples, and reds. The birds' chorus gives way to songs of the night's insects. The home glows from within its many windows. Changing seasons in the garden always bring new delights. Spring ephemerals, such as Virginia bluebells, prairie smoke, and May apples, appear briefly and then retreat backstage for next year's cameo roles. Summer presents Jensen's favorite prairie roses, majestic Queen of the Prairie, down-to-earth bluestem grasses, and copious coneflowers, which then entice flocks of goldfinches and the fast flicker of migrant hummingbirds. Fireflies spark amidst the waving grasses in July, and insects hum so loudly you can hear their buzz a block away. In autumn, every plant offers a poignant adieu, from burgundy oaks to flaming sumacs. Winter showcases moonlight, softly backlighting the mighty bur oak at the corner of the lot and then gracefully arcing to a gentle glow above the river. Snowfall, typically scorned in our hardened Chicagoan hearts, is welcome in this garden, making light of downtrodden branches and wispy flower heads. Ice freezes in crystalline sculptures from Wright's angular, open downspouts. "Gutterspout" seems like such a harsh word for these artful ornaments; let's call them waterspouts, for their orchestral dance of flowing water during a rainfall is a sight and sound to behold.

Goldfinches and other birds enjoy the prairie gardens beside the Gardener's Cottage.
Photo by Jerry Kumery, 2005.

Prairie plant "puppet shows" enliven the plaster walls and pyramidal ceiling in the Gardener's Cottage living room. Photo by the author, 2005.

The cottage's smooth, stucco surface outside serves as a blank canvas for nature's show of light and shadow. Photo by the author, 2005.

Bees collect pollen from the garden's native plants, such as this coneflower.
Photo by the author, 2005.

*Monarch butterflies are among the insects enjoying the monarda in
the prairie garden. Photo by the author, 2005.*

*A young bird finds refuge in a mass of Northern sea oats in the cottage's prairie garden.
Photo by the author, 2005.*

Native plants, such as serviceberry, offer year-round interest with spring blossoms and summer fruit. Photo by the author, 2005.

Compass plants in the cottage's prairie garden offer color and interest.
Photo by the author, 2005.

The view toward the Gardener's Cottage from Coonley Road, across the sunlit opening or "clearing." Photo by the author, 2005.

*Sunrise from across Olmsted's triangle of greenery filters through
the Gardener's Cottage's many windows. Photo by the author, 2005.*

Sunset paints the sky behind the Gardener's Cottage.
Photo by the author, 2009.

A rainbow forms over the Gardener's Cottage after an early morning rain.
Photo by the author, 2005.

Then there is the sky. Before finding the Gardener's Cottage, we had lived in all four quadrants of Riverside, and rarely did we see the sky. It is, perhaps, one downside of our leafy village; with smaller lots and, of course, their large, precious trees, glimpses of the wide-open sky are rare. The little Gardener's Cottage—sited at the base of the hill, on a corner lot, and open to Olmsted's triangle of greenery—frames the clouds of day and stars of night. To be sure, it isn't Montana's big sky, but it's an impressive little clearing amidst the sheltering branches and leaves of trees. During summer, from the bench at the north end of the garden, or in winter at the hearth, we watch the sun set behind a latticework of oaks, as it has for more than a century for those fortunate to live in a "small masterpiece presented by three great American titans," Frank Lloyd Wright, Jens Jensen, and Frederick Law Olmsted: the Gardener's Cottage, in Riverside, Illinois.

NOTES

In Their Nature

1. Elizabeth Coonley Faulkner, as quoted in a *Washington Post* interview, April 19, 1981.

2. Marcia L. Woodhams, as quoted in www.sil.si.edu/SILPublications/seeds/seedsmanbios.html (accessed December 1999).

3. Queene Ferry Coonley to Dexter M. Ferry, Jr., 27 January 1933, Ferry Family papers, Bentley Historical Library, University of Michigan.

4. The cottage school began in the Whittlesley cottage on the estate grounds. This was an existing stone cottage built in approximately 1894 by the Louis Sullivan-trained architect, Charles Whittlesley. Thorncroft, the home built by William Drummond across from the Gardener's Cottage, was built to house teachers for the Cottage School. The Coonleys built a school in nearby Brookfield, Illinois, and another in Downers Grove, Illinois. The Avery Coonley School in Downers Grove remains one of the Chicago area's leading independent schools.

5. John Dewey and Evelyn Dewey, *Schools of Tomorrow* (1915; New York: E. P. Dutton & Co, 1962) 66–67.

6. Queene Ferry Coonley, "Come let us live with our children," *Progressive Education* (1927). While Coonley's Brookfield school was also located on a creek, the references to the Indian lore, French explorers (i.e., the nearby historic Chicago portage), and description of the flowering riverbank more strongly suggest that this was the original Riverside Cottage School and workshops.

7. John Stuart Coonley, *Chronicles of an American Home* (New York: J. J. Little & Ives Co., 1930).

8. Ibid.

9. Q.F. Coonley to D. M. Ferry, Jr., 15 April 1912, Ferry Family papers.

10. D.M. Ferry to Q.F. Coonley, 29 March 1905. Ferry Family papers.

11. John Stuart Coonley and his wife lived on Cornell Avenue, according to the 1900 U. S. Census.

12. Q. F. Coonley to Jeannette and Dexter M. Ferry, Jr., 11 April 1933. Ferry Family papers.

13. The 1904 move is referenced in the *Riverside News*, April 2, 1920. 1910 U.S. Census records show the Howard Coonleys living on Delaplaine Avenue, although notes in the Frank Lloyd Wright archives (Frank Lloyd Wright Preservation Trust, Oak Park, Illinois) say Howard Coonley moved to the Munday house on Michaux Road. Howard Coonley may have moved to Riverside rather than the North Shore, like brother Prentiss, to be near the family's enamelware factory on Chicago's West Side. The Howard Coonley family moved from Riverside to Boston in 1913, according to the *Riverside News*, October 2, 1913, which reported, "Mr. and Mrs. Coonley have been some years with us and are leaving many friends who regret their removal." Note also that, while there was a D. W. Ferry living in Riverside in 1912, he was a distant relation, not Queene Ferry's brother, who only lived temporarily in the estate during September 1918, while the Coonleys were in Washington, D.C. (D. M. Ferry to Q. F. Coonley, 28 October 1912; Avery Coonley to Major D. M. Ferry, 18 September 1918, Ferry Family papers.)

A Meeting of the Minds

1. *Riverside News,* February 1913. Avery Coonley was part of an early movement to keep Riverside free from alcohol.

2. *Riverside News*, January 30, 1913. The article refers only to Mr. Kellogg; presumably, it is Charles Kellogg, given the descriptions and era.

3. *Riverside News*, June 5, 1913.

4. *Riverside News*, October 28, 1915.

5. *Riverside News*, n.d.

6. Elizabeth Coonley was listed as a field marshal for the society, whose president was Mrs. Henry Babson, of Riverside's Louis Sullivan-Jens Jensen designed Babson Estate. Catherine Mitchell, a locally renowned naturalist, was secretary-treasurer. *Riverside News*, May 7, 1914.

7. *Riverside News*, May 7, 1914.

8. Happily, these homes are still extant, although they are repurposed. Milfer Farm (see www.milferfarms.com) is a state-of-the-art facility for raising thoroughbred horses, and it includes 600 acres of fenced pasture and cropland. Hillside, in Wyoming, New York, has been transformed to the Hillside Inn, a luxurious American country inn (www.hillsideinn.com).

9. Q. F. Coonley to D. M. Ferry, 4 May 1920, Ferry Family papers, Bentley Historical Library, University of Michigan.

10. *Riverside News*, April 2, 1920.

11. Frank Lloyd Wright and Jens Jensen, contemporaries each with strong views and personalities, worked on only a handful of projects together. Scholars point out that these efforts were not true collaborations with simultaneous give-and-take, but rather sequential designs in which one preceded the other. Robert Grese cites four Frank Lloyd Wright/Jens Jensen clients besides the Avery Coonleys: Sherman Booth, of Glencoe, Illinois (1911–1912); Abby Beecher Longyear Roberts, of Marquette, Michigan (no date); William Greene, of Aurora, Illinois (1912), and Prentiss Coonley, of Lake Forest (1910–1911). See Grese, *Jens Jensen, Maker of Natural Parks and Gardens* (Baltimore: The Johns Hopkins University Press, in association with the Center for American Places, 1992).

12. Frank Lloyd Wright to Avery Coonley, 24 September 1906, Frank Lloyd Wright Archives, Frank Lloyd Wright Foundation.

13. Q. F. Coonley to D. M. Ferry, Jr., 4 May 1911, Ferry Family papers.

14. F. L. Wright to Q. F. Coonley, 27 June 1935, Frank Lloyd Wright Archives.

15. F. L. Wright to Jens Jensen, 1 March 1943, Frank Lloyd Wright Archives.

16. Elizabeth Coonley Faulkner to Carol Doty, 12 May 1974, Sterling Morton Library archives at The Morton Arboretum, Lisle, Illinois.

The Gardener and His Wife

1. Riverside's local directory, for instance, lists Avery Coonley, but not his wife, despite her high social profile, prominent public works, and Ferry family fortune.

2   Spellings are approximate, based on the author's best interpretation of the handwritten documents.

3. William Drummond to Avery Coonley, 21 October 1919; A. Coonley to W. Drummond, 16 October 1919, Frank Lloyd Wright Preservation Trust Archives, Oak Park, IL. Note that Coonley spelled "Thornecroft" with an "e," which is missing in many of today's publications.

4. *Chicago Heights Star*, October 31, 1933.

5. Q. F. Coonley to D. M. and J. Ferry, 17 August 1916, Ferry Family papers, Bentley Historical Library, University of Michigan.

6. Q. F. Coonley to D. M. Ferry, 21 October 1901, Ferry Family papers.

7. Q. F. Coonley to D. M. Ferry, 19 January 1903, Ferry Family papers. Although no surname is provided, the author infers that this Archie is Archibald Gill, based on other references in the Coonley-Ferry letter exchanges.

8. D. M. Ferry to A. Coonley, 22 June 1911, Ferry Family papers.

9. A. Coonley to D. M. Ferry, 24 June 1911, Ferry Family papers.

10. D. M. Ferry to A. Coonley, 23 September 1911, Ferry Family papers.

11. A. Coonley to D. M. Ferry, 9 September 1911, Ferry Family papers.

12. Q. F. Coonley to D. M. Ferry, 29 July 1912, Ferry Family papers.

13. One persistent historical rumor in Riverside lore has it that the Drummond cottage, built in approximately 1913, was intended to handle the gardener's expanding and overflowing family. The author has found no evidence that the Gills ever had any children. We do know that one of Archie's brothers was available to help at the estate during 1911. Perhaps this accounts for the notion of an expanding family. According to another source, since the Drummond cottage was built around the time Thornecroft was built for the Cottage School teachers, another caretaker for the teachers' building lived in the Drummond cottage. Perhaps when Jens Jensen prepared landscape plans for the Coonleys, the gardening demands became too great for Archie, and additional gardeners were hired.

14. Interestingly, Queene Ferry Coonley writes of first meeting Mrs. Vaughan in 1916 at a resort in La Jolla, California. "She is a lovely type of woman, fully interested in outdoors things along the lines of their business interests." Q. F. Coonley to D. M. Ferry, 1 March 1916, Ferry Family papers.

15. A. Coonley to D. M. Ferry, 11 July 1915, Ferry Family papers.

16. *Riverside News*, July 8, 1915.

17. Q. F. Coonley to D. M. Ferry, 18 June 1932, Ferry Family papers.

18. Q. F. Coonley to D. M. Ferry, 30 October 1933, Ferry Family papers.

19. Cemetery records show that, in 1935, Archibald Gill paid for a contract for internment in the cemetery's columbarium. It is unclear whether this was for the remains of his wife, Susan, who died two years prior, or a prepayment for himself. The nameplate on the columbarium niche reads only Susan Gill, with her birth and death dates. Cemetery officials are puzzled by this mystery but confident that the remains of both Gills are located there.

Leaving the Riverside Villa

1. Q. F. Coonley to D. M. Ferry, 8 September 1917, Ferry Family papers.

2. The Coonleys continued to admire Frank Lloyd Wright, and the Prairie Style, even though their home at Rosedale was decidedly more traditional. They suggested commissioning prairie architects Dwight Perkins or William Drummond for the family home in Milfer, though Drummond did not, apparently, appeal to Jeannette and D. M. Ferry, Jr., in developing plans for their own home.

3. Q. F. Coonley to Blanche Hooker, February 19, 1915, Ferry Family (Dexter Ferry) papers, Bentley Historical Library, University of Michigan.

4. *Poughkeepsie New Yorker*, March 17, 1954, from the Vassar College Alumnae Clipping Service.

5. A. Coonley to W. Drummond, 16 October 1919, Frank Lloyd Wright Preservation Trust.

6. "Beautiful Coonley Home Sold," *Riverside News*, April 2, 1920.

7. A. Coonley to W. Drummond, 16 October 1919, Frank Lloyd Wright Preservation Trust. Also, Whittlesley is often spelled Whittlesey in various publications.

8. Q. F. Coonley to D. M. Ferry, undated, Ferry Family papers.

9. Q. F. Coonley to D. M. Ferry, 12 April 1920, Ferry Family papers.

10. Q. F. Coonley to D. M. Ferry, 23 April 1920, Ferry Family papers.

11. Frank Lloyd Wright to Peter Kroehler, 26 September 1929, Frank Lloyd Wright Archives, The Frank Lloyd Wright Foundation.

12. F. L. Wright to Mrs. P. Kroehler, 4 June 1951, Frank Lloyd Wright Archives, The Frank Lloyd Wright Foundation.

13. Celia Crawford, telephone interview with the author, 12 May 2005.

14. *Washington Post*, June 21, 1923.

15. Ibid.

16. *New York Times*, July 11, 1958.

17. Peter Kroehler had two other children from a previous marriage, Delmar and Gladys, who lived elsewhere with their mother, Josephine Stevens Kroehler.

18. "The Symphonic Poem of a Great House," *House Beautiful* (November 1955): 322.

Be It Ever So Humble

1. Frank Lloyd Wright, *An Autobiography* (New York: Longmans, Green and Company, 1932), 164.

2. Charles E. Aguar and Berdeana Aguar, *Wrightscapes: Frank Lloyd Wright's Landscape Designs* (New York: McGraw-Hill, 2002), 117.

3. The Gardener's Cottage was included on Wright's original plans, including those printed in the Wasmuth Portfolio. It is believed that actual construction began on the cottage sometime later. Construction dates of this building and the others are approximated as follows, in William Storer's *Frank Lloyd Wright Companion* (Chicago: University of Chicago Press, 1993): Main residence (1907), original Gardener's Cottage (1911), stables (1911), Thornecroft (1912), Thornecroft Caretaker'sCottage (1913), and playhouse (1912).

4. Carolyn and the late Jim Howlett, respectively a professor in the School of the Art Institute of Chicago and a professional photographer, are largely credited for saving the Coonley estate, after they bought and remodeled the former stables in the 1950s.

5. Wright built a gardener's cottage for the Darwin Martin house in Buffalo, New York, in 1904. Like the Coonleys, the Martins were avid gardeners—their estate included a conservatory, and a "floricycle" landscape element planted by Walter Burley Griffin. The Darwin Martin gardener's cottage, however, while sympathetic to the estate's architecture, was across the street from the main complex, built of stucco instead of brick like the rest of the estate, and it included two full stories of living space. With these early designs for the workingman, one wonders if Wright was developing his Usonian designs.

6. Virginia Henry, interview with the author, July 12, 2004.

7. Here, on a modest scale, Wright's original design afforded the privacy of a "secret entrance" to the gardener. Virginia Henry recalls that the front steps leading from the sidewalk to the porch were hidden by a low cement wall (about 2½ to three feet). The current covered entrance was added in the 1950s, and the two-tiered cement front stoop was added in the 1990s. Interestingly, the Gardener's Cottage always had its own private sidewalk leading to the front door. While the gardener wouldn't have had a driveway to his house, this separate walk still would have pleased Queene Ferry Coonley, who once wrote, "I vote on [a] separate sidewalk. I always do feel neglected when walking up a driveway. It is different on a country road but in a city and a formal entrance I do like a place for people separate." (Q. F. Coonley postscript to note from A. Coonley to D. M. Ferry, 14 November 1912, Ferry Family papers, Bentley Historical Library, University of Michigan.) How might this preference have influenced the compromise design on the main estate, where a pedestrian path borders the driveway to the main residence?

8. One of the missing windows opened into the porch area, and the other was on the opposite side of the room, lost during the bedroom addition in the 1960s.

9. One of the Gardener's Cottage windows is now displayed in the Musee d'Orsay, France.

A Landscape Legacy

1. "Beautiful Coonley Home Sold," *Riverside News*, April 2, 1920. On Olmsted's plan, Riverside lots were grouped into divisions. The First Division included the peninsula of land surrounded by the bend of the Des Plaines River.
2. From the online herbarium hosted by the Morton Arboretum of Lisle, Illinois, at www.vplants.org.
3. This wall was removed in the 1950s.

ABOUT THE AUTHOR

CATHY JEAN MALONEY is a senior editor at *Chicagoland Gardening* magazine and is the author of *The Prairie Club of Chicago* (Arcadia Publishing, 2001) and *Chicago Gardens: The Early History* (The University of Chicago Press and the Center for American Places at Columbia College Chicago, 2008).

Born and raised in the Chicago area, Ms. Maloney received a B.B.A. from the University of Notre Dame and a M.B.A. from Northwestern University. Following twenty-two years at Andersen Consulting (now Accenture), Ms. Maloney's career developed in the field of garden history and writing. Her articles on gardens and landscape history have appeared in numerous magazines and newspapers, including *Better Homes and Gardens*, *Gardens Illustrated*, *Landscape Architecture*, *The Public Garden*, the *Chicago Sun-Times*, and the *Daily Herald*. She has also taught at the Chicago Botanic Garden and University of Chicago Graham School of General Studies and writes for The Morton Arboretum in Lisle, Illinois.

ABOUT THE BOOK:

The Gardener's Cottage in Riverside, Illinois: Living in a "Small Masterpiece" by Frank Lloyd Wright, Jens Jensen, and Frederick Law Olmsted is the fourteenth volume in the *Center Books on Chicago and Environs* series, George F. Thompson, series founder and director. The book was brought to publication in an edition of 1,000 hardcover copies with the generous financial support of the Friends of the Center for American Places, for which the publisher is most grateful. The text was set in Adobe Garamond Pro and the sidebars in Ministry. The paper is Chinese Gold East matte, 157 gsm weight. The book was printed and bound in China. For more information about the Center for American Places at Columbia College Chicago, please see page 110.

FOR THE CENTER FOR AMERICAN PLACES
AT COLUMBIA COLLEGE CHICAGO:

George F. Thompson, Founder and Director
Brandy Savarese, Editorial Director
Jason Stauter, Operations and Marketing Manager
Erin F. Fearing, Executive Assistant
Purna Makaram, Manuscript Editor
Abigail Friedman, Book Designer
David Skolkin, Art Director

The Center for American Places at Columbia College Chicago
600 South Michigan Avenue
Chicago, Illinois 60605-1996, U.S.A.
www.americanplaces.org

Distributed by the University of Chicago Press
www.press.uchicago.edu

17 16 15 14 13 12 11 10 09   1 2 3 4 5

Library of Congress Cataloging-in-Publication Data

Maloney, Cathy Jean.
      The Gardener's Cottage in Riverside, Illinois : Living in a "Small Masterpiece"
by Frank Lloyd Wright, Jens Jensen, and Frederick Law Olmsted / Cathy Jean
Maloney. — 1st ed.
      p. cm. — (Center Books on Chicago and Environs)
Includes bibliographical references and index.
ISBN 978-1-930066-89-2 (alk. paper)
1. Gardener's Cottage (Riverside, Ill.) 2. Architecture, Domestic—Illinois—
Riverside. 3. Coonley, Avery, 1870-1920—Homes and haunts—Illinois—
Riverside. 4. Coonley, Queene Ferry—Homes and haunts—Illinois—Riverside.
5. Wright, Frank Lloyd, 1867-1959. 6. Riverside (Ill.)—Buildings, structures,
etc. I. Title. II. Series.

NA7238.R58M35 2009
728'.37097731—dc22
                                                        2008044110

ISBN: 978-1-930066-89-2

Center for American Places

AT COLUMBIA COLLEGE CHICAGO

THE CENTER FOR AMERICAN PLACES at Columbia College Chicago is a nonprofit organization, founded in 1990 by George F. Thompson, whose educational mission is to enhance the public's understanding of, appreciation for, and affection for the places and spaces that surround us; that is, the natural, built, and social landscapes of the world—whether urban, suburban, rural, or wild—with an emphasis on North America. Underpinning this mission is the belief that books provide an indispensable foundation for comprehending and caring for the places where we live, work, and commune. Books live. Books endure. Books make a difference. Books are gifts to civilization.

Since 1990 the Center for American Places at Columbia College Chicago has brought to publication more than 330 books under its own imprint and in association with numerous publishing partners. Center books have won or shared more than 100 editorial awards and citations, including multiple best-book honors in more than thirty fields of study.

For more information, please send inquiries to the Center for American Places at Columbia College Chicago, 600 South Michigan Avenue, Chicago, Illinois 60605-1996, U.S.A., or visit the Center's Website (www.americanplaces.org).